*Journeymen*

# Journeymen

## A Spiritual Guide
## for Men

*(and for Women Who Want to Understand Them)*

KENT IRA GROFF

UPPER
ROOM BOOKS™
NASHVILLE

JOURNEYMEN: A SPIRITUAL GUIDE FOR MEN
(AND FOR WOMEN WHO WANT TO UNDERSTAND THEM)

All scripture quotations unless otherwise noted are from The New Revised Standard Version of the Bible, copyright © 1989 by the Division of Christian Education of the National Council of the Churches of Christ in the United States of America. Used by permission.

Scripture quotations noted as AT refer to Author's Translation of the text based on the original languages of scripture in Hebrew or Greek. Those noted as AP refer to Author's Paraphrase.

Scripture quotations identified as KJV are from The King James Version of the Bible.

Scripture quotations identified as RSV are from The Revised Standard Version, copyright © 1946, 1952, 1971 by the Division of Christian Education of the National Council of the Churches of Christ in the United States of America. Used by permission.

Scripture quotations identified as NIV are from the Holy Bible, New International Version. Copyright © 1973, 1978, 1984 International Bible Society. Used by permission of Zondervan Bible Publishers.

Excerpt from *John of the Cross*, edited and introduction by Kieran Kavanaugh, O.C.D. © 1987 by the Washington Province of Discalced Carmelite Friars, Inc. Used by permission of Paulist Press, Inc.

"Healing" by D. H. Lawrence, from *The Complete Poems of D. H. Lawrence* by D. H. Lawrence, edited by V. de Sola Pinto & F. W. Roberts. Copyright © 1964, 1971 by Angelo Ravagli and C. M. Weekley, Executors of the Estate of Frieda Lawrence Ravagli. Used by permission of Viking Penguin, a division of Penguin Putnam, Inc., and Laurence Pollinger Limited and the Estate of Frieda Lawrence Ravagli.

Excerpt from "The Way of Pain" from *Collected Poems 1957–1982* by Wendell Berry. Copyright © 1985 by Wendell Berry. Reprinted by permission of North Point Press, a division of Farrar, Straus & Giroux, Inc.

Lyrics from "Scarlet Begonias" by Robert Hunter. Used by permission of Ice Nine Publishing Co.

"Snake" from *House of Light* by Mary Oliver. © 1990 by Mary Oliver. Reprinted by permission of Beacon Press, Boston, Mass.

Interior design and layout: Nancy J. Cole
Photograph: John Kelly/The Image Bank © 1999
Second printing: 2000

*Library of Congress Cataloging-in-Publication Data*

Groff, Kent Ira.
 Journeymen: a spiritual guide for men and for women who want to understand them / Kent Ira Groff.
  p. cm.
 ISBN 0-8358-0862-9
 1. Christian men—Religious life. 2. Christian life.
 3. Spirituality. I. Title.
 BV4528.2.G756 1999
 248.8'42—dc21

   98-41300
   CIP

Printed in the United States of America

*In gratitude*
*for healing memories of*
*my parents, Francis and Mary,*
*and my brother, David*

# Contents

# Index of Prayer Exercises

# Index of Resources

# Acknowledgments

Writing in solitude is possible for me only because of a rich community of family, friends, and mentors. I am grateful for ideas that emerge in conversing with individuals and groups. So I especially want to acknowledge some of the friends who read and commented on all or parts of *Journeymen*, giving me valuable insights: Nancy Agneberg, Mark Altschuler, Dr. Stephen Boyd, Stephen Bretsen, Dr. Jeffrey Buckwalter, Rabbi Carl Choper, Bishop Michael Creighton, Elena Delgado, Dr. Arthur Goldschmidt, Dr. Elizabeth Groff, Fredrika Groff, Kendra Groff, James Groff, Mary Hodges, Timothy Jones, Phyllis Lindquist, Ray I. Lindquist, Dr. David McFarlane, Glenn Mitchell, Dr. Karl Ruttan, Br. Robert Sevensky and novitiates at Holy Cross Monastery, West Park, New York, James Walkup, and Cynthia Wickwire.

I appreciate the invaluable interaction with other apprentices and mentors as I presented themes of *Journeymen* at Princeton Theological Seminary, New Jersey; Union Congregational Church (UCC), Upper Montclair, New Jersey; Chautauqua Institution, New York; Wayne Presbyterian Church, Wayne, Pennsylvania; United States Penitentiary, Allenwood, Pennsylvania; Presbyterian Men 1996 national meeting; and Oasis Ministries, Camp Hill, Pennsylvania. I also thank students and colleagues at Lancaster Theological Seminary, Pennsylvania, for many fruitful conversations and feedback. And I thank my editors, JoAnn Miller and Karen Williams, for their encouragement, guidance, and affirmation.

More valuable than any printed book is learning to read the books already written in one's heart. I depend on others for the chance to hear myself make connections between ideas of the mind and sometimes long-forgotten drops of experience—my own or another's. When those connections occur, a healing of the soul takes place.

—Kent Ira Groff

# Introduction

## Farther

"I'd like you to meet
my farther," he said.
But the embarrassing "r"
revealed a truer core:
the father he had
never really met
and the frightening spheres
between them,
a lonely distance
concealed in years
of dis-appointments:
"We'll get together then." [1]

After a period of silence during a retreat, Joel told his small group the following story:

> It was late on a hot afternoon in a M★A★S★H unit during the war in Vietnam, and my duty was to help triage the wounded. Among the bloody young men, there appeared a perfect one, beautiful, serene. Only one problem: On further examination, there was this one tiny hole in his chest. He was dead. That experience changed me. I had always wanted life neat, organized, perfect. But I decided I'd take it messy, bloody and alive rather than neat, perfect—and dead.

*Journeymen* is about "men on a journey," engaged in a risk-taking spiritual adventure. It is also about journeymen in the classic sense: an apprentice who has completed his training and is now on the way to becoming a mentor for other journeyers. These are the two major themes of this book.

1. "Men on a journey" implies that one has not yet arrived, so it is countercultural in Western society that values productivity over process, task over relationship. Like the man who was wounded while going down from Jerusalem to Jericho (Luke 10:25-37), every man experiences some wounding on the way to his destination. The classic male

wound of an emotionally absent father or father figure—as portrayed in the opening poem—can be as damaging as a wound from physical or sexual abuse. And you do not need a traumatic experience like Joel had in Vietnam to realize that a subtle internal wound can be more deadly than another person's visible wound.

2. I am also using *journeymen* in the classic medieval sense: young adults who have completed their apprenticeship and have begun the craft of life. But to become whole and stay whole, at some point an apprentice needs to become a mentor. Alcoholics Anonymous and other Twelve-Step groups have understood this incredible mystery: A key to successful sobriety is to become a sponsor for another. Like the "Good Samaritan" who in Luke's story had experienced rejection, if we are in touch with our own painful experiences, we can use them to empower others rather than to hurt or ignore them. An important task of this male journey is to move from cool indifference (like the robbers, priest, and Levite in the story) to embrace our pain, to acknowledge our wounded feeling function as a source of a new kind of power. Those who can do this will be the real heroes in twenty-first-century culture.

## Ideas and Experiences: The Warp and Woof of a Male Tapestry

The basic skill in practicing this craft of faith is to connect our isolated human stories with the divine Story. When I began working on *Journeymen*, I knew I had to use stories and that some of the stories had to be mine. What emerged is an integration of spiritual ideas and life experiences woven like a tapestry, so that in looking at a variety of ideas, the same color threads will reemerge as we explore the warp and woof created by this oscillating shuttle of being men, being Christian.

I recognize the value of spiritual autobiography, yet part of me resists using my own stories. Always there's the danger of self-absorption. I recall how John Killinger was once asked if he thought it was OK for ministers to use personal stories in their sermons. He paused, then replied, "Yes—it's all right so long as the stories put the preacher in the position of needing grace."

I have found three compelling reasons to take the risk to use my own stories. First, Christian faith is embodied spirituality: "The Word became flesh and lived among us" (John 1:14). If people are going to be drawn to a Christ who is real, it will not be an intellectual Christ, but One who lives and breathes through human beings in whom they see themselves. Men, who are often left-brain "thinkers," need a Christ who makes sense to the mind *and* heart, and story does just that. I hope the stories from my life and others will trigger your own memoirs, so the Word becomes flesh in your life.

Second, the sheer weight of precedent is on the side of writing about one's own story-journey: the Apostle Paul, converted from persecutor to proclaimer (Acts 9:1-19; 22:6-21; Gal. 1:13-24); Augustine, playboy turned bishop, penning his *Confessions*; John Wesley, whose "heart was strangely warmed" at Aldersgate in London; Corrie ten Boom, risking death by the Nazis while smuggling Jews to safety in *The Hiding Place*; Frederick Buechner, in all his writings speaking of his father's suicide, and in *Telling Secrets*, revealing his daughter's anorexia.

Stories create a sacred middle ground because they provide a safe vehicle to disclose our feelings, thus connecting us with other men but also with the women in our lives who yearn to understand us. (Most stories in this book are told anonymously; otherwise the names have been changed to preserve confidentiality.)

There's yet a third reason for the frequent use of personal story, reflected in a statement which I keep in boldface, uppercase letters on my computer screen to catch my attention as I write:

### WRITE YOUR WAY HOME!

Each of us is always working—
writing, drawing,
drafting, designing,
laughing, crying,
plowing, mining,
sweating, writing—
playing and praying our way home.

John Cheever said he wrote to make sense out of life. Danish philosopher Søren Kierkegaard said, "Life must be lived forward, but it can only be understood backwards." Weaving stories with ideas trains my eye to see the thread of providence running through the crazy stuff of life. (See Rom. 8:28.)

## Journeymen: Model for Male Spirituality

*Pilgrimage* implies struggles along the way. Christ is "the Way"—the journey itself (John 14:6), and followers of the Way are called to a life where obstacles are transformed into opportunities (Acts 9:2; 24:14).

*Journeymen* speaks of friendship; an ordinary companion on our journey may be the Messiah concealed in human guise (Luke 24:13-35; Matt. 25:31-46). "I have called you friends, because I have made known to you everything that I have heard from my Father" (John 15:15). It is a call for men to model Jesus' radical friendship to each other and the world.

As the term *journeyman* conveys an apprentice-mentor relationship, Christ is the true Mentor: "Take my yoke upon you, and learn from me; for I am gentle and humble in heart" (Matt. 11:29). This kind of mentoring is the genuine imitation of Christ: "Be imitators of me, as I am of Christ" (1 Cor. 11:1; see also Phil. 2:5-11; 3:17; 1 Thess. 1:6-7; 1 Peter 2:21).

But no one has ever lived *now* before, so this journey calls us to be companions and apprentice-mentors for each other. How shall we then live—as men? as believers? as human beings?

What about men and work and men and death? These two themes are so present in male experience that I have chosen to weave them throughout the entire book. All the time guys risk death for "success."

## Notes about the Layout of the Book

I have interspersed two kinds of brief transitions between chapters to change your vista before journeying on:
- An *excursion* is a brief side trip to explore a concept or an idea.
- A *reststop* is a place to pause and meditate on some drop of human experience.

Each is related to the previous and the following chapters, yet easy to read on the run and self-contained enough to be used as a brief devotional reading for individual or group use.

At the end of each chapter are Prayer Exercises, primarily for personal use, though some are adapted to group use, and so noted. At the end of each chapter are questions for Personal Reflection or Group Discussion, which sometimes draw on the Prayer Exercises. The intent of these is to create laboratories of experience where spiritual transformation can take place for active people. Many times I will refer to the Resources in the back for personal or group exercises. (See index.)

When I use "you" in a sentence, it is not finger-pointing, but speaking personally as to myself in my journal: You need to trust God in this very moment, redeeming these very moments.

## Four Ways to Use the Book

1.  You may read *Journeymen* as an individual, praying, using a journal, and deepening your companionship with God. Even so you will probably find yourself sharing bits and pieces with others.

2.  You may read it along with a friend, using the reflection questions and Prayer Exercises to share informally by phone, by e-mail, or in person. If you live near each other, you might covenant more formally as spiritual friends or prayer partners, to meet together monthly or semimonthly.

3.  The book is ideal for group study. If you are part of such a group, see if members would consider developing one-on-one spiritual friendships (prayer partners) as an ongoing practice during the weeks of using this study book. (See 2. above and Resource IV.)

4.  You may also develop a men's retreat drawing from the meditations, prayer exercises, and themes of the book.

Making use of a spiritual journal will increase the benefits of all four methods. So if you do not have one, I encourage you now to purchase a simple book to assist your apprenticeship. (See Keeping a Journal, page 138.) While some may prefer to journal using a computer, there is still great value in also having a traditional "longhand" journal where you jot notations of scriptures, poetry (your own or others'), art, dreams—or your own psalms and prayers. I will be coaching you with many "props" along the way, with special notations in the Prayer Exercises for using the journal.

**1**

# Journeymen

## An Orientation

Now is the time for all good men to come to the aid of the party.
—Charles E. Weller

Back before this politically correct era, many of us were trained to use the above jingle to count the number of words per minute we could beat out on a real typewriter. But now *is* precisely the time for *men* to address some of our own unique spiritual, sexual, and vocational issues for the sake of *all* parties concerned, women and other men, wives and companions, sons and daughters, parents and friends, colleagues and enemies—the world.

*Men are in crisis.* One young adult who read this statement wrote in the margin, "We are?" After pondering his comment, I went to a lecture by Brother Andrew of Holy Cross Monastery, a Benedictine community in West Park, New York. A native Scot, he told how in Celtic tradition men reluctant to express emotion would *sing* their feelings. It was not unusual in a family gathering for someone to suggest, "Let's have a wee concert." Then everyone, even Uncle Bobby or Aunt Maggie, who could not carry a tune, would contribute some bit of music, others stomping a foot, humming along. Or after supper, a wife would say to her husband, "Ah, darlin', sing to me." And he would grunt, "Nah"—but later proceed to croon, "Your love is the reddest rose. . . ."

Whatever your background—African, Native American, Middle Eastern, European, Asian, Jewish, Hispanic—the rituals where the majority of men were singers, drummers, harpists, poets, dreamers, storytellers and pray-ers have been largely squeezed out by our Westernized way of life and work.

So the crisis is subtle, yet obvious. Men still die sooner than women of a myriad of health-related, stress-related causes, even in Japan, where they have the highest longevity rate. And in the United States, heart attacks, the number-one killer, strike at a significantly higher rate among men, and at one time of the week—Monday mornings, a telltale sign concerning men and work.[1] We fall in love and father children at alarming rates without knowing how to love them or their mothers. In *Boys Will Be Boys: Breaking the Link Between Masculinity and Violence*, Myriam Miedzian asserts that of all violent crimes 89 percent are committed by men; that 1.8 million women suffer physical assault by husbands or boyfriends annually; and that the number of men who are murdered is triple the number of women.[2] And, I would add, most of us "responsible" men sell our souls to our work without knowing why, then die early of physical problems related to our loneliness.

This is not male bashing—it is reality in the postindustrial, postmodern, technological world. In the past our elders were our mentors. But since no one has ever lived in the twenty-first century before, our elders cannot say to us, "This is what it's like."

## Out of Crisis: A Collage of Opportunity

Many of us grew up with a picture of what life would look like, even if it was an idealized picture. But now all we have are torn fragments of our pictures. What is required is a new art form, let's say, a *collage* of these fragmented traditions of family, spirituality, vocation, sexuality, values.

But at the very time when we are experiencing this major fragmentation, we are also losing the glue and the backboard for the collage! That's the real crisis. The spiritual bonding for this new configuration—the lost stories, myths, ballads, prayers, rituals—must be refashioned if we are to create a meaningful collage out of these scraps of yesterday's black-and-white snapshots and today's color prints.

Just as the word for "crisis" in Chinese (and many Asian languages) is composed of two separate word-symbols—one character representing "danger" and the other "opportunity"—we can choose to view the crisis in male identity as an occasion for spiritual emergence.

The Greek word *krisis* in John's Gospel is translated "judgment," referring to Jesus' cross, his hour of crisis. Just as Moses lifted up the dangerous serpent on a pole in the wilderness and it became a sign of healing, so the Child of Humanity must be lifted up on a cross (John 3:14). This "lifting up" simultaneously embodies the meanings of Jesus' crucifixion and his exaltation into heaven. Today the ancient serpent on a pole is the caduceus symbol that you still see in physician's offices. Jesus as the Child of Humanity absorbs life's venom and lifts it up to be transformed.

The cross is the end of this one solitary life, yet it is transformed as a doorway to life eternal for all. In T. S. Eliot's words, "to make an end is to make a beginning." This is the good news we need to hear when coming to the end of a marriage, the end of a career, the end of any relationship. This is the good news for men, for women, for loved ones, for enemies.

The gospel means that if we "lift up" our most destructive dangers to conscious awareness, praying them instead of suppressing them, the crisis can become a window of spiritual opportunity. Prayer is the laboratory of transformation where we actualize this good news. Prayer means entering the photographic darkroom and lifting up our crises to the Light, so the negatives can become the source of positive prints.

With training in the darkroom of prayer, we can be journeymen photographers! Then we can become mentors for others whose hidden treasure may be the negatives of their lives—if only they knew it! People are looking for journeymen apprenticed in the art of lifting up life's emergencies to become occasions for spiritual emergence.

Now we are back to our twenty-first-century collage. Together we can apply the spiritual bonding of our stories and begin creating a new collage that represents the transforming Presence among us. What we get from the laboratory of prayer may be only fragmented photos (chapter 9). For this collage we need the varied background materials from folk arts, classical arts—country music, rock, jazz, movies, plays, poetry, fiction—to create rituals where the mundane and profane stuff of life can be "lifted up" in our time. To discern means to train the eyes of the heart to see glimpses of new life in our thwarted opportunities (chapter 10). As the lyrics of Robert Hunter in "Scarlet Begonias" express it, "Once in a while / you get shown *the light* / in the strangest of places / if you look at it right."

## Women's and Men's Perspectives

Just recently I walked into a large bookstore of a national chain and asked for their section on men's issues. The manager told me there was no such section, but that a few men's books were scattered under subtopics like sexuality, work, and self-help. This is despite the fact that the store had a big section on women's issues and that I was aware of scores of contemporary books on men's issues. The paltry "scattering" of men's literature belies our impoverished fragmented male souls. Sam Keen laments a similar experience in *Fire in the Belly: On Being a Man*.

The burgeoning area of feminist studies, and womanist studies among African American women, is a call for men to pay special attention to our unique issues. Kim Post, who conducts diversity programs for businesses and nonprofits, noted this urgency in a recent lecture at Chautauqua, New York. Mentioning how many books tell women how to relate to men, but how few tell men how better to relate to women, she said, "Men want to reclaim their humanity, and women want to claim their full powers. This is an opportunity for us to be allies or mentors to each other, for women know how to have relationships and men know how to exercise power." Yet I need to add that for *some* men or *some* women it can work the other way around!

The so-called mythic-poetic men's movement draws on ancient myths of the world with books like Robert Bly's *Iron John and* Robert Moore and Douglas Gillette's *King, Warrior, Magician, Lover*. *Journeymen* is meant to be a bridge between this movement and the evangelical Promise Keepers. I find a hunger for biblical moorings that integrate *being men* with *being Christian*, yet in such a way that preserves dignity and diversity. That is what this book is about.

Women are reclaiming unique metaphors of faith and identity from the Bible, literature, and myth, often buried in the centuries-old bastion of dominative male theology and culture. All of us, men and women, are enriched by this process.

For example, the feminine scriptural image of "sufferings as birth-pangs" helps me to conceive of personal or cosmic struggles as divine labor pains giving birth to new life (Rom. 8:18-28; John 16:20-22; Matt. 24:8). Male theologians of the mystical tradition often used such integrative images. Meister Eckhart, for example, spoke of God as generative, and how "giving birth" always involves disturbance. As I experience the struggles and joys of writing this book, of founding and directing a nonprofit organization, I am sustained by the image of giving birth.

The metaphor of God as "Birth-giver" suggests the human role of being a midwife. Paul wrote to the Galatians, "My little children, for whom I am again in the pain of childbirth until Christ is formed in you" (4:19). Genuine spiritual metaphors need look in both directions: Who is God (theology) and how shall we then live (ethics)?

*Journeymen* provides such a model for male spirituality: Christ is the true Mentor; we are apprenticed journeymen becoming mentors.

## In Search of a Model for Male Spirituality

A young man was quoted in an interview, "Men are like microwaves and women are like Crock-Pots." The problem for many of us is that these generalizations just do not work. Reading John Gray's *Men Are from Mars, Women Are from Venus*, my wife and I found more examples of where she was from Mars and I was from Venus! (For example, some men talk a great deal, and not all women are like waves, whose self-esteem crests and falls.) What a great number of men need is a way to move beyond the psychological boxes of male and female, to discover how to integrate the polarities of life in a way that creates a distinctive collage of male spirituality.

Some insist that the only means for healing the male soul is to believe in and pray to a male Father God.[3] Surely I want to reclaim Father as one primary name for God, as Roberta C. Bondi advocates in *Memories of God*, because for Jesus *Abba* embodied qualities of intimacy and compassion. And with Diane Tennis I answer the question in her book title *Is God the Only Reliable Father?*—Yes![4] Today's political correctness can get in the way of spiritual needs. Recently I heard the sad story of a man who had trained himself not to refer to God as Father. Then when this man's father died, he desperately needed to cry out to God as a Father, but could not give himself permission to do so. So any human metaphors of God can be limiting or distorted.

As a male in a world of fast-changing careers, I need God as *Abba*, the father who reveals the trade secrets to the son (Matt. 11:27; Luke 10:22). Yet as a male I am also nurtured by God as Mother: "the Rock that bore you . . . the God who gave you birth" (Deut. 32:18; see also Isa. 51:1-2; 66:13; Matt. 23:37). As a child born of a mother in her forties and in frail health, I want God as my Rock Mother!

I need an integrative spirituality: the gentle strength symbolized by Aslan the Lion who represents Christ in C. S. Lewis' children's series The Chronicles of Narnia. I need a "severe mercy" (to use another Lewis image) that cuts through the sexist nonsense and sets me free to embrace my vulnerable side as strength and pay attention to the seismic fissures in my powerful side.

*Journeymen* provides a model of men becoming aware of unique wounds we have received *and* given along the way, then rising to return and find in our vulnerability a source to empower self and others.

## A Male Spirituality? Two Modes of Experience

So if one rejects the simplistic stereotypes of male and female, is there a unique male spirituality? I have been asked this many times and still struggle with the issue.

First, I take a clue from biblical stories of male siblings like Cain and Abel (Gen. 4), Jacob and Esau (Gen. 25-33), and the Prodigal and the Perfectionist (Luke 15:11-32). From these I learn that there is no one-size-fits-all male mode of experience, but rather a spectrum. The one end may be described as the dominative or assertive male mode, and the other as the impoverished or passive male mode. Often the two do battle in the same person, as in the story of Thomas Watson Jr. (chapter 7). The genuine male soul integrates and balances both of these in a healthy way.

In an unhealthy form, Cain kills his brother Abel. Much male violence results from rapid flipping from feeling impoverished to striking out at the world. The expression "flipped out" conveys an abrupt reaction. Like the late comedian Flip Wilson's old line, "The devil made me do it!"—that is what happens when you lose your center and surrender to your worst self: You blame others and deny responsibility. Spiritual maturity is to move from uncontrolled "flipping" to discerning a creative use of passiveness and of assertiveness.

Second, I am convinced that both nature (male physical anatomy) and nurture (Western culture) do in fact give men a unique tendency toward outward and linear modes of being in the world. So the key to men's wholeness lies in balancing our natural dominative propensities by shutting down our mental computers and descending inward to listen to our hearts *before* there's a crisis.

The Christ of the Gospels is the model of this holistic integration—retreating to the desert to pray, getting interrupted, then going forth, "Let us go on to the neighboring towns . . . for that is what I came *out* to do" (Mark 1:35-38; italics mine). In a redeemed form, the righteous or integrated man needs the spiritual balance of going out (healthy assertiveness) and returning (healthy passiveness). There are unique male ways of maintaining this balance (chapters 10–12).

Third, studies of men's and women's brains show that men and women process information differently: men more rapidly but separately in left and right spheres, women more gradually back and forth. This would indicate that we males need not only to make use of our rapid responses but also (a) to discipline ourselves to cultivate silences to allow time to integrate information in the two spheres of the brain, and (b) to call on the community to discern a variety of options. (See chapter 8, page 106.)

The Bible is full of stories about men that highlight this reality: that if we do not stop to listen to life and the community, life will stop us. We will explore some key parables of Jesus that portray the balance of the soul's going out (descent, or separation) and returning (ascent, or reintegration). In the story of the Good Samaritan, a man journeys "down" a dangerous road, is wounded, and then is "raised up" on a beast and brought to an inn—home while on the journey (Luke 10:25-37). The Prodigal Son journeys to a far country, gets "down" with the pigs, then comes to himself, rises to return home (Luke 15:11-32). This pattern of descending, rising, and returning is embodied in the church's liturgy: "Christ has died. Christ is risen. Christ will come again."

Such woundings can become a means of gentling our raw male power—like breaking in a horse. Aslan the Lion, the Christ figure in C. S. Lewis's Narnia series, is a prototype of gentle strength. We see this same deep truth in Goethe's *Novelle* where the lion (Dionysian energy) is gentled through the piping of a little child (Apollonian energy). And in Revelation, Christ is simultaneously the Lion and the Lamb.

> Strength without gentleness is brutality;
> gentleness without strength is sentimentality.

If a man's task-oriented, "warrior" side is already highly developed, he needs to pray to integrate the kinder, gentler side of Aslan; he will still be a lion, but one with *gentle* strength. Or a man may have a highly developed "lover" side—these are often males in the helping professions, such as teachers, ministers, social workers, counselors, and many musicians and artists and writers. Then one's task is to make friends with the "warrior" side of Aslan, developing gentle *strength*.

## Rock Water

> Light casts
> heavy shadows
> while soft water
> over hard rock
> splits time—
> in its own time.

> Tremble, O earth, at the presence of the LORD, . . .
> who turns the rock into a pool of water,
>     the flint into a spring of water.
> (Psalm 114:7-8)

## PRAYER EXERCISE 1: Solitude and Community

I invite you to meditate on the scripture in Mark 1:35-39, where Jesus retreats to the desert to pray—and is interrupted. Ponder the rhythm of solitude and community in Jesus' life. Using your journal or notebook, assess this balance of *being* and *doing* in your own life. (In assessing your spiritual disciplines, be challenging yet gentle on yourself.) Conclude with an inward mental prayer or write a prayer.

## PRAYER EXERCISE 2: Gentle Strength

"Strength without gentleness is brutality; / gentleness without strength is sentimentality." Which is more likely your sin—brutality (distorted strength) or sentimentality (distorted gentleness)? Which area do you need to cultivate? What would your life look like with more balancing of these? Pray and ponder, inwardly or using your journal.

## For Personal Reflection or Group Conversation

1. What are the problems and benefits of defining such a thing as "male spirituality"?

2. What do you think of the two modes the author proposes—the dominative/assertive male and the impoverished/passive male? What are some healthy and unhealthy aspects in each mode? What aspects of these do you see in yourself or your family of origin?

3. Reflect on your responses to Prayer Exercise 2. How would you apply this to some aspect of your present situation—in your work, family, community, or church? Notice varied perspectives among your colleagues.

# EXCURSION 1:
## Roads and Highways

Road: a strip of ground over which one walks. A highway differs from a road not only because it is solely intended for vehicles, but also because it is merely a line that connects one point with another. A highway has no meaning in itself; its meaning derives entirely from the two points that it connects. A road is a tribute to space. Every stretch of road has meaning in itself and invites us to stop. A highway is the triumphant devaluation of space, which thanks to it has been reduced to a mere obstacle to human movement and a waste of time.

Before roads and paths disappeared from the landscape, they had disappeared from the human soul: man had stopped wanting to walk, to walk on his own feet and to enjoy it. What's more, he no longer saw his own life as a road, but as a highway: a line that led from one point to another, from the rank of captain to the rank of general, from the role of wife to the role of widow. Time became a mere obstacle to life, an obstacle that had to be overcome by ever greater speed.

Road and highway; these are also two different conceptions of beauty.

In the world of highways, a beautiful landscape means: an island of beauty connected by a long line with other islands of beauty.

In the world of roads and paths, beauty is continuous and constantly changing; it tells us at every step: "Stop!"

—Milan Kundera, *Immortality*[5]

You would not build your home on an expressway. You cannot even enter the world of a corporation from a fast-moving interstate, but have to exit and usually backtrack a bit to find the road to company headquarters. Yet Western society is addicted to the expressway lifestyle of "onward and upward," exporting it around the world. I confess I often choose to drive expressways, yet they could certainly be made more interesting and with little damage to the environment.

The Taconic State Parkway, which runs inland parallel to the Hudson River in New York State, is an example: beautiful stone bridges, curves, and wide medial strips landscaped with trees and rock outcroppings.

In contrast, the US 322 bypass around State College, Pennsylvania, split the outlying village of Oak Hall in two—for the sake of maintaining a straight line. How many times does a man (or woman) allow an addiction to a straight line of career or success to split family, friendships, or even a nation (as in the case of a dictator)—or one's own life? A curve might be less boring and keep the traveler from falling asleep and having an accident. In baseball, the curve ball is an art.

Instead of this "Damn the torpedos—full speed ahead"[6] attitude, the authentic male journey is open to curves and twists and wasted space for beauty. It is a spiritual pilgrimage, each new arrival marking the beginning of yet another pathway. "And Abram journeyed on by stages toward the Negeb" (Gen. 12:9).

The mountain trailblazer knows the value of gentle switchbacks to break the assault of a deadly precipice. Milan Kundera is right: "In the world of roads and paths, beauty is continuous and constantly changing; it tells us at every step: 'Stop!'"

Your journey with this book will take you on a few "excursions," like this one, to explore the meaning of a single idea, a word, a place, a concept of God or of human life. Like Kundera's concept of "roads" and "highways," such excursions will be mainly left-brained, theological, reasoned.

We will balance these by pulling aside for a few "reststops"— where the object will be to pause along the road and look more carefully at some drop of human experience, "To see a world in a grain of sand," using William Blake's phrase. The reststops will be brief story-meditations that are a bit more right-brained, intuitive, experiential.

It is my hope that this side trip has spawned inner connections with your own spiritual pilgrimage. I hope the reststops and future excursions will do the same.

# Jacob's Ladder

## Process vs. Task

> It is precisely the soul that is the traveler; it is of the soul and
> of the soul alone that we can say with supreme truth that
> "being" necessarily means "being on the way" (en route).
>
> —Gabriel Marcel, *Homo Viator*

I remember visiting a man from New England who became critically
ill on the Pennsylvania Turnpike. From the hospital bed he mentioned Jack Kerouac's classic book and said, "Everything significant
happens to me on the road." Kerouac's title illustrates the popularity
of the theme. As I write this forty-some years since its publication in
1957, *On the Road* still sells more than 100,000 copies a year!

### Journey and Home: Creative Balancing

*Journey* conveys a linear and exterior movement, and as such is a "masculine" archetype, that is, a universal pattern of experience. Its counterpart is *home*, a more culturally "feminine" archetype, an interior
metaphor—men's "shadow," or less developed side. Each archetype
functions in both men and women; in differing ways we all yearn for
security and adventure. As Russell Banks reportedly stated about *Rule
of the Bone*, "All travel books are really about finding home."

In the Twenty-third Psalm, the two images are dovetailed. The
journey leads through all sorts of circumstances: green pastures, paths
of justice, still waters, and through the valley of the shadow of death.

Then the scene shifts to the image of home: a table spread, an anointing blessing, an overflowing cup, in God's house and heritage forever. God is present as both Shepherd and Companion on the journey—a masculine image, and as Host at the table—a feminine image. For as conservative biblical scholar Kenneth Bailey has pointed out, Who in Middle Eastern culture would prepare the table but a woman?

We see the creative paradox of these two themes in the mystical writings of John of the Cross, and those of his spiritual counterpart, Teresa of Avila. John's famous poem, "The Dark Night," is based on a journey away from the house: "One dark night . . . / I went out. . . ." In contrast, the great theme of Teresa's classic book title, *Interior Castle*, expresses the inward metaphor of home.

Yet Teresa's work is also about a journey—an interior pilgrimage cycling into the soul's deepest center, mansion by mansion. And John's work is also about home: having left the house, the soul "comes home" in an intimate rendezvous with God while on the path into the night.

Greek female-male archetypes of journey and home are portrayed in the classic masterpieces *The Iliad* and *The Odyssey*, attributed to Homer. Odysseus is the absent father/war hero, and his wife, Penelope, represents the faithful creative presence of home and hearth, while their infant son, Telemachus, is entrusted into the care of Mentor. But an even more difficult odyssey than Odysseus's Trojan War exploits is his ten-year attempt to return home to his son through endless wanderings and hardships. *The male soul's attempt to return to his heart is far more difficult than any career exploits.*

Obviously women also learn from the exterior world, just as men learn from the interior world. Split from each other the two modes are not only sexist, but dysfunctional! Men and women have both archetypes within them, and the art of becoming integrated is to make friends with the shadow side of the self: "So God created humankind in [God's] image, . . . male and female [God] created them" (Gen. 1:27). In Hebrew tradition this text portrays God as both male and female, and every human being likewise embodies masculine and feminine qualities.

Exaggerating home can lead to stagnation or confinement; exaggerating journey can lead to exhaustion or invasion. Yet each can be balanced in a paradoxical way: Home can become a daring adventure through embarking on the inward journey. And the outward journey can become a royal road within by pausing to notice homecomings along the way, as the following story of Jacob's stopover at Bethel illustrates.

## Jacob's Ladder: Linear and Cyclical

[Jacob] came to a certain place and stayed there for the night, because the sun had set. Taking one of the stones of the place, he put it under his head and lay down in that place. And he dreamed that there was a ladder set up on the earth, the top of it reaching to heaven; and the angels of God were ascending and descending on it. And the LORD stood beside him and said, "I am the LORD, the God of Abraham your father and the God of Isaac. . . ." Then Jacob woke from his sleep and said, "Surely the LORD is in this place—and I did not know it!"

(Genesis 28:11-13, 16)

Many of us grew up singing "We Are Climbing Jacob's Ladder" in summer camp. The ladder image in this text is often criticized because it would seem to reinforce a macho desire for control to achieve upward mobility. It may even be used to reinforce unhealthy images of male sexual anatomy in our technological culture: The computer is "up" if it is working, "down" if its malfunctioning. Sensitive women and men in Western society are conditioned by "a man's world" and must deal with the painful tension created by an aggressive, ladder-climbing lifestyle.

Of course certain personality types are more task oriented— whether male or female—while others are process oriented, as the popular Myers-Briggs Type Indicator (MBTI) illustrates. Are these tendencies gender based, environmental, personal, or cultural?

*Whatever the basis, males in Western culture generally value productivity over process.* What is sad is that it is assumed to be a necessary trait for men and women if they are to survive in the world of management anywhere—business, finance, health care, education, even church! The subtle image of an invisible "glass ceiling" that keeps women from moving upward is a telltale sign that society has been conditioned by this hierarchical and linear worldview.

But actually Jacob's ladder is countercultural. What is overlooked in this story is that the angels of God are ascending *and* descending on it—taking it out of the purely ladder-climbing sequence and creating an integrative image. *Jacob's ladder is linear but also cyclical:* "And [Jacob] dreamed that there was a ladder set up on the earth, the top of it reaching to heaven; and the angels of God were ascending and descending on it" (Gen. 28:12).

"Angels" meet us on our ladder-journey as we are being lowered and raised again and again! In the only other direct reference to Jacob's ladder in the Bible, Jesus says: "You will see heaven opened and the angels of God ascending and descending upon the Son of Man" (John 1:51).

Jesus embodies the paschal mystery of the paradox of death and resurection that is woven into the very fabric of the universe, nature's cycles of devastation and renewal.

For the dominative male to "see heaven opened" he needs to pay special attention to angels on the descent, while the passive male needs to pay special attention to angels on the ascent. I invite you to pause and notice such times.

## The Cross: Model of Falling and Rising

In Raymond Carver's story "A Small Good Thing," Howard Weiss reflects on his life as he drives home in the rain from the hospital. There his son, Scotty, lies in a coma after being hit by a car that very morning on his eighth birthday. Howard ponders:

> Until now, his life had gone smoothly and to his satisfaction—college, marriage, another year of college for an advanced degree in business, a junior partnership in an investment firm. Fatherhood. He was happy and, so far, lucky—he knew that. His parents were still living, his brothers and his sister were established, . . . So far, he had been kept away from any real harm, from those forces he knew existed and that could cripple or bring down a man if the luck went bad, if things suddenly turned.[1]

Here is expressway living: a straight line onward and upward. Of course it is fiction. Yet all men, and many women, are controlled to a great degree by the fantasy of this ideal trajectory. The obsession with "success" has a debilitating effect on those who do not achieve it, and even those who attain it want more.

Back at the hospital, counterpointing Howard's ascent is the rhythm of descent: He watches Scotty's "small chest quietly rising and falling under the covers." During the next days the parents' expectations are raised and lowered like a yo-yo. In the end, when Scotty has died, his mother "could feel [the doctor's] chest rising and falling evenly against her shoulder."

At home after Scotty's death, the grieving parents explode over a bizarre series of anonymous phone calls implying they do not care about Scotty. In a moment of revelation, Ann Weiss realizes it has been the baker all along—harassing them for not picking up Scotty's birthday cake. At midnight, the couple heads for the bakery: Ann's anger intensifies, rising to rage. She's ready to kill.

But during the encounter the baker begs forgiveness and in the process discloses his own emptiness and childlessness. Mysteriously the couple's rage gives way to a cathartic experience of talking out their grief amid the smells of rising bread. There has been a blessing in this innate rhythm or rising and falling: "Just as suddenly as it had welled in her, [Ann's] anger dwindled." The mother and father sit in the bakery, conversing with the childless baker into the early hours of the morning, "and they did not think of leaving."

"Eating is a small good thing at a time like this," says the baker, whose own misplaced anger at Ann and Howard has also dwindled. What began as a violent mission to kill the baker has been transformed into communion. The stony heart of anger turned to bread.

## Growing Up, Growing Down

The God of Bethel redeems the upward *and* downward movements in our lives, the expanding and dwindling, times for growing up, times for growing down. We can never go beyond the paschal mystery, only deepen it. Jacob's ladder is a pattern for male spirituality integrating loss and failure with gain and success.

What had been only a stopover along the road the night before, with a few hard stones for a pillow, has now become Bethel—house of God. Jacob prays to go out and to return, "If God will be with me and will keep me in this way that I go, and will give me bread to eat and clothing to wear, so that I come again to my father's house in peace" (Gen. 28:20). Always there's a return and reintegration: "Christ has died, Christ is risen, Christ will come again."

In the return is the seed of reconciliation and reintegration: as with Howard and Ann Weiss and the baker, and with the angry parts of themselves; as with Jacob's return to his father's house, which leads to reconciliation with his brother Esau; as with the return of the Prodigal, which leads to reconciliation with his father.

We journey out and risk death and exhaustion, we rise, and return again and again to the presence of God and "see the heavens opened and the angels of God ascending and descending" on this human Messiah (John 1:51). This is what it means to be "in Christ." The journeying out *and* coming home, the ascent and the descent, are integrated in a continuous linear-cyclical experience.

## Rx for the Male Ascent: Silence, Prayer, and Retreat

But as men we get trapped on the ascent and assume the only way upward is to control. There's nothing more disastrous than for a sensitive personality type like myself to try to be aggressive. There's a fine line between being assertive and being aggressive, and when I cross that line I can feel it going against my own grain. I know because I have tried it many times, both in management and family contexts.

When I was pastor of a church and conflict broke out among members spilling over into staff relationships, aggressive executive types in our denomination told me how to take charge, act tough, be the boss. When it did not work (because it will not if you try to act out of someone else's ideal rather than act out of your unique self), these folks just told me I tried their strategy too late.

But it was like putting King Saul's armor on young David, who said to Saul, "I cannot walk with these; for I am not used to them" (1 Sam. 17:39). It was giving a relational man the tools of a hierarchical man. My style of power is more collaborative and horizontal, theirs more hierarchical and vertical. One type is not always better than another, and each needs some corrective: It is a question of balance and being true to oneself.

In reaction to my own fear of being vulnerable, I became brittle. Afraid of being goalless, I flipped to the opposite. Reacting (instead of responding) is the one form of "macho" sin common to both the dominative and the passive male. In my flailing from one to the other was my failing. I became goal driven when what I needed was to be goal free. Instead of trying to manipulate the situation, I needed to shut down my internal computers—stay with and pray with my passivity and listen to what God might be saying in each lived moment on that perilous journey.

It would have been so helpful back then if I had had a spiritual companion (in addition to a therapist), a soul friend to meet with me, like Jonathan who "strengthened [David's] hand through the LORD" (1 Sam. 23:16). I needed a Jonathan to love me "as his own soul," to listen, to pray at these painful junctures of my journey (20:17, RSV). But I did not even know there was such a thing and certainly did not know how to create it! A trained spiritual guide could have helped me slow down: to stop, to contemplate these acid drops of experience in the laboratory of the presence of God and another. Within each concentrated drop of one's experience is what I call *a hologram of meaning* which, if we pay attention to it, contains a parable for one's entire journey.

Freed from *my* controlling methods to achieve *my* goal, I could have been open to a destiny—freed to gain new skills that would tap into my own unique collaborative, nonhierarchical strengths to achieve God's intention. *What I needed was to reframe the goal as God's liberating destiny. Instead I became addicted to my controlling destination.*

GO

Risk

Play

Do good

Give love

Journey out

Live as if you had a thousand years to live

Live as if you you were to die tomorrow

Return home

Receive love

Trust God

Pray

Rest

BE

## "Go . . . I Will Show You . . . by Stages"

What would happen if as males we simply shifted the goal from *destination* (which *I* can achieve, plan, and control) to *destiny* (where *God* invites me to a future I cannot yet see, beyond my control)? (See Excursion 2 at end of this chapter.)

Abraham's journey presents a model for the male spiritual journey: "*Go* from your country and your kindred and your father's house to the land that *I will show you.* . . . And Abram journeyed on *by stages* toward the Negeb" (Gen. 12:1, 9; italics mine). Here's an unfolding journey with three requirements: first, courage to venture outward and risk one's security; second, trust that God will reveal the ultimate destiny; and third, patience to journey by stages to each short-term destination. "For here we have no lasting city" (Heb. 13:14).

*To be whole, we need to learn the art of being open to continual homecomings while still on the road.* Ponder the difference between a pressured business trip and a relaxed pleasure trip to the Holy Land. In the first, one's mindset is to arrive at the destination on time for the appointments to accomplish the tasks. But in the second, if you have only the mindset to arrive at Jerusalem by a certain time, you'll allow no space to enjoy the famous sites along the way: Nazareth, Jacob's Well, Jericho, Khirbet Qumran, Bethlehem, Rachael's Tomb.

The authentic male pilgrimage is a clarion call to appreciate the journey itself with its obstacles and surprises, without being addicted to a destination. To pause in this very moment and surrender your premapped destination is to become open to God's liberating destiny for you.

Often women in the gospel stories can teach us men about that less-developed side of our male selves. The women who come bearing spices to anoint Jesus' body instead find the tomb empty: Their goal is thwarted; his body is not there. Yet by having the courage to enter the darkness, face their grief, and leave the tomb empty, they encounter the living Lord outside the tomb, farther down the road! By having the courage to enter the empty spaces of our life, we can emerge to see the obstacles of the journey itself as opportunities for growth.

*To ask, How is God inviting me to respond (instead of react) to this problem? already changes the problem itself.* Every human dilemma becomes a divine invitation. "[P]rayer, not the existence of God, is the thing to be decided," Patricia Hampl reflects in *Virgin Time: In Search of the Contemplative Life.* Prayer is the spiritual response we make to the outward circumstances of life.

How can we begin moving from mechanical reaction to spiritual response? By cultivating silent pauses for prayer and solitude, you can begin to see that the wounds you have received (and woundings unwittingly given) are precisely the openings for grace. It is the magic of the discipline of solitude—coupled with the discipline of community: the two components of a journeymen group. (See chapters 11 and 12.) *And that is why those apprenticing to be journeymen need space and time for mentors to teach this craft of faith from the art of their experience of life with God.*

## PRAYER EXERCISE 3: Angels on the Ascent

Read the text of Genesis 28:10-16. Ponder some "upward" movements in your life, some high points, achievements. Notice one where it seems to you that God has been actively present, affirming you through people or experiences. In a journal or notebook, begin to express the feelings, relish the taste of joy in them. But also be attentive to any downside connected to this joy, and offer it to God as you move to Exercise 4. Write or sing a prayer of thanksgiving.

## PRAYER EXERCISE 4: Angels on the Descent

Reread the text of Genesis 28:10-16. Ponder some "downward" movements in your life, experiences of loss, diminishment—people, places, events. Focus on one, and begin to notice the pain in it. Then, also begin praying, asking yourself, *Has there been any gift in this experience for me?* In a journal or notebook, begin to express the feelings of pain in the descent. Continue writing—then see if you can reach the place of expressing some gift(s) out of this experience. Try writing a prayer that offers both the feelings of pain and thanksgiving.

## For Personal Reflection or Group Conversation

1.  If you meet with a group or a friend, devise a way (one-on-one is usually more comfortable) to share experiences based on Prayer Exercises 3 and 4 above.

2. "What would happen if as males we simply shifted the goal from *destination*?" How would you pray differently? What would it mean to apply this to a specific situation in your setting?

3. In the story of the baker, Ann Weiss's anger wells up, then dwindles. She had been ready to kill. What are some clues to her change of heart?

4. "To ask, How is God inviting me to respond (instead of react) to this problem? already changes the problem itself." How do you see the difference between *reacting* and *responding*?

# EXCURSION 2:
## Destination and Destiny

The poet Mary Oliver writes that words often sound like what they do. How do the words destination and destiny sound different? When I set out to write this book, I had no conscious awareness of any difference between destination and destiny. But as I began writing, while staying with my wife at the Prince of Peace Abbey in Oceanside, California, the words began to sound different to me. After reflecting on it with Fr. Luke, my on-the-journey Benedictine spiritual director, my ponderings sent me scurrying to the abbey library to see if there was any linguistic basis for my intuitive distinction. A Benedictine monastery would be the right place to find a good Latin dictionary! Sure enough, I found several.

Both words come from the Latin de-+stenare (from the same root as the Latin word stare), literally "to cause to stand." But it can also mean "to fasten down, to make secure." One of the definitions for destiny is "the purpose for which something or someone is intended; ultimate design."

Aha! I had found it now—or I should say it had found me! Destination fastens your life down, promises security. Destiny causes you to stand up and claim the original design for which you are intended. I recalled Archimedes' rubric: "Give me where to stand, and I will move the earth!" What a powerful image of destiny! And I recalled how in the New Testament the primary word for Jesus' resurrection in Greek is anastasis—"standing."

Later I wanted to check out my newfound combination of intuitive knowledge and logical research. So I asked my wife, "How do these two seem different to you?" Instantly she answered, "When I think of destination, I think of short term. When I think of destiny, I think of long term, lifetime!"

Voilà! There it was. Macho spirituality attaches to penultimate destinations and makes them ultimate. Short-term destinations control us. This is what addictions do: They rob us of our journey itself while kidnapping our deeper, long-term joy. When we embrace genuine *male* spirituality on the other hand, we can relinquish the short-term fulfillments to God while still being open to claim our lifetime destiny! Genuine male spirituality frees us to enjoy the penultimate destinations without being addicted to them. Even our mistaken destinations, like mirages in the desert, can lead us to the source of ultimate joy in God. Hence the Catholic expression *Felix culpa!*—"O fault most fortunate!"

Some days later I asked my two daughters the difference between destination and destiny. The younger answered: "Concrete and abstract." The older answered: "Oh, they're completely different. One is about where you're going, the other is about what gets you there." Like good Eastern riddles, there's a lot here to ponder. We become addicted to our destinations and when they disappoint us, we have lost a piece of our soul.

Yet God can use the concrete destinations if we offer them—even the addictions, whether to substances or to work, even to good things. And in a moment of becoming aware that the journey is not about these short-term fulfillments, they can be transformed into a source that lures us toward our long-term destiny.

Weeks later, rummaging through my teaching notes for a course on vocation, I found the following quotation in my handwriting—maybe from a student, maybe from the synergy of a mutual student-teacher insight:

*God weaves our destiny out of the threads of the choices we make!*

# Samaritan Journeymen
## The Male Wound

In the middle of the journey of our life
I came to myself within a dark wood
Where the straight way was lost.
> —Dante, *Inferno* I: 1.1

Contemplative prayer keeps us home, rooted and safe, even when we are on the road, moving from place to place.
> —Henri J. M. Nouwen, *In the Name of Jesus*

If I want to get home I've gotta give somebody else a ride.
> —Anonymous Folk Saying

"A man was going down from Jerusalem to Jericho," and when a man's mind is fixed on a destination, it is nearly impossible to listen. "Going *down*" foreshadows his descent. It is high-risk behavior to travel alone, especially on a known dangerous way. We know the rest of story: "And [he] fell into the hands of robbers, who stripped him, beat him, and went away, leaving him half dead" (Luke 10:30). Yet this stubborn risk-taking is also a man's gift to lead him unawares to a wound which will become the source of a new kind of strength.

But right now, the goal is not to get from Jerusalem to Jericho— nor *to* anywhere, because you might rush there and be found half dead and not know where you are. The words of the Cheshire-Cat to Alice in *Alice's Adventures in Wonderland* are right—that if you don't care where you're going, it doesn't matter which road you take. If you continue to make *your* destination rather than *God's* destiny your focus, sooner or later you will encounter obstacles and wounds that will stop you dead in your tracks. It may be ulcers or alcohol, a debilitating illness, a career or family crisis, or just a gnawing emptiness.

Of course it is not so simple; if you knew for sure you were following your own destination and not God's destiny, you would change courses! Here is a clarion call to men to exercise the self-discipline of taking a time-out on the journey right now! *Do not wait for the next external wounding to beat you to the draw and rob you of life and leave you half dead.*

The main reason we do not take time out is that we are scared to death of the past wounds that will surface if we do. During a brief half-day retreat in Hershey, Pennsylvania, I had directed the group in a half an hour of silent prayer. During a discussion I suggested taking a more extended silent retreat, an overnight and a day, at the Jesuit Spiritual Center in nearby Reading. One pastor retorted that he could never imagine going away for even a day in silence because, "I'm scared to death of what I might discover in myself." The bandits had already knifed him, and he was afraid to look at his wounds.

## Male Wounding: Through Circumstances or Choice

Actually the robbers have already been there and beaten every one of us to the draw. If you are a man, then you have already experienced the male wound. It is there within us in some form: a crystallized experience of absence or failed intimacy with a father or a father figure.

We will explore the sources of that wound now (chapter 3) and forms it can take (chapter 4); then the fear and anger that result from this wound (chapter 5); and some ways of "pouring on oil and wine" (chapter 6).

The Good Samaritan story (like that of the Prodigal Son) is about men—though it is *not* solely for *men*. It illustrates two sources of the male wound. In one sense, this "journeyman" on his way from Jerusalem to Jericho is wounded by his own inner choice. He does a foolish thing by setting out on a known dangerous road (we court risks), and alone (we are fiercely independent). In another sense, his wounding is a result of circumstances beyond his control. Robbers attack him unjustly (just when we try to "get it right") and by surprise (stuff happens).

Woundings from foolish risks we take are more *macho*; a prodigal young adult deliberately journeys to a "far country" and lives recklessly. Woundings inflicted through circumstances of victimization are more *innocent*; a child is thrust with no choice into a family and is sexually abused; a company downsizes and a guy is left jobless. Children, minorities, and women experience more of the latter, yet both sexes experience both. All of us get hurt, sometimes by our own lousy choices, sometimes by chance, other times by a combination of bad fortune and foolish actions. How does this apply to the male wound?

## Male Identity: Who You Are vs. What You Do

This story of the Good Samaritan is actually about a journeyman with no identity!

As men we most often begin our journey anonymously, lacking a sense of self—yet we are very clear about our outer destination. A boy is programmed early to know where he is going before he knows who he is.

What do you want *to do* when you grow up? And even if the question is asked, What do you want *to be*, the answer expected invariably has to do with career—teacher, scientist, politician, musician—not character—Christian, philanthropist, compassionate person, creative person. Julia Cameron in *The Artist's Way* makes the point that Western culture belittles the art of creativity.

To put it more pointedly, the less we know about who we are, the more hell-bent we will likely be on "getting somewhere" by the world's standards because that is precisely where we find our identity: in arriving somewhere, financially, academically, socially, politically, even spiritually. In her excellent short book, *The Spiritual Life*, Evelyn Underhill says, "We mostly spend [our] lives conjugating three verbs: to Want, to Have, and to Do."[1]

Like this nameless journeyman, we set out from our Jerusalem to our Jericho with no identity but with a clear arrival point. Paul Tillich said that before sin is an act, it is a state of being. So if we do not know who we are, our best actions will arise out of a nameless self and may blindly harm self and others. Jesus made this clear: "For it is from within, from the human heart, that evil intentions come" (Mark 7:21).

Another way of looking at this classic parable is to suggest that the man really did not know who he was or where he was going. He may have made up his mind to go Jericho for no good reason, like George Leigh Mallory, who risked the dangers of Mount Everest "because it is there." A man will frequently fall into any kind of risky destination that has nothing at all to do with his destiny—but he will do anything in the world rather than stand still and learn from life, or journey inward to find out who he is.

Former President Richard M. Nixon and President Bill Clinton, in very different ways, represent the tragedy of brilliant men driven by misplaced destinations and addictions. Was it an addictive fear of losing control for Nixon, instead of surrendering his creative gifts to be drawn, Quakerlike, from his roots toward his true destiny? Has President Clinton suffered from an addiction to power-over relationships and a fear of being alone? For each, the Achilles heel was his cover-up, a lack of courage to risk being vulnerable at the outset of the sin. How much was this fear related to the distant- and absent-father wounds of their childhoods? Had each been courageous enough to journey inward, he might have spared great harm to himself, his family, and the nation. The mystical scientist Blaise Pascal wrote in his *Pensées*:

> When I begin to think about the various activities of men, the danger and troubles they face at court, or in wartime—which are the source of so many quarrels and violence, wild and often evil adventures as well—I have often felt that the sole cause of man's unhappiness is that he does not know how to stay quietly in his own room.[2]

But our society is addicted and economically codependent on its insatiable thirst for scandal and violence. Every one of us needs to hear Pascal's plea. So it is not that males in Western society have no identity, but that we are programmed to find our identity in the wrong places—in money, sex, degrees, achievements, power! Good things become our masters. The dominative male sells his soul for these outward attachments, and the impoverished male feels soulless, and his desperate way to get these things is to lash out. Both souls are lost.

Yet salvation means receiving one's true identity in God, not from the world: "Do not fear, for I have redeemed you; / I have called you by name" (Isa. 43:1). This book is about salvation: about allowing

God to call you by name, which means to embrace your soul's particular genetics and twisted environment, to commit to be your unique self right now, and forever. Only with that self-awareness and self-acceptance can you hope to give back a bit of unconditional heaven to our twisted society.

That is why Martin Luther King, Jr., echoing his mentor Mohandas Gandhi, said that the content of a person's character has power beyond class or color. It is not that your "name" has to be perfect, but that you can embrace your true self because your name is written in the palms of God's hands (Isa. 49:16). (See Prayer Exercise 6.)

## The Robbers, the Priest, and the Levite

"Now by chance a priest was going down that road; and when he saw him, he passed by on the other side. So likewise a Levite" (Luke 10:31-32). Actually, each character in this story is part of us. At first blush, the robbers and the religious guys may seem like opposites. But if you look closely, both have numbed their feelings to any responsibility—both represent the passive impoverished male.

It is easy to see this in the priest and the Levite. Literally, they cannot offer help; to touch blood would disqualify them from their duties. To "get it right" politically and religiously, each one must steel his feelings and walk by on the other side. In the name of duty the destructive passive male shadow leaves the spirits of people half dead, even in our best institutions, while killing people's bodies in wars.

But the dominative attack of the robbers also comes out of their desperate passivity. A counselor working with serial killers tells how the perpetrator does not feel anything, thus resorting to more and more violent acts. These people describe themselves as the living dead. Said one of the atrocity he committed, "I did it to see if I would feel anything."

Passive violence can seem less raw. I remember arriving one morning well before the early Sunday service at the church I was serving. While I was filling the baptismal font, an usher (who I knew would soon move to a new home) bounded toward me to "confess" how he had declined to rent his present house to an African American family. I recall feeling his helplessness, and my own, yet being grateful for his awareness and vulnerability. Standing at the baptismal font, I think what I said was that God would forgive him, but that he had better be careful not to miss the next chance he would be given to act on the courage of his convictions. How easily we flip from control to paralysis.

This is why *not* knowing and embracing who you are can project hell onto society. The German psychologist, Alice Miller, wrote about a man who had been abused as a child. For the least little offense, actual or imagined, his father would beat him. He did not even call his son by name. Instead he whistled for him like a dog. Feelings of hatred boiled deep within the boy, but never expressed, they become rage. Sometime later the son discovered that his father's father had been Jewish. His distorted logic led him to blame his father's behavior toward him on this Jewish blood.[3]

You know this boy's name: Adolf Hitler. And you know his death-dealing story. Who knows if healing one male wound might prevent a future cosmic holocaust?

And now we have come to the deepest level of the male wound: failure of a father by his presence to confer the blessing of identity on a child—and the fear this absence creates within the person and within the systems of which they are a part.

*So the sin resulting from our foiled identity is not that men seek power, but that we seek the wrong kind of power and from the wrong sources.* It is about pursuing power that controls others out of fear in the name of security, instead of power that empowers others and self out of love.

## The "Good" Samaritan

"But a Samaritan, as he journeyed, came to where he was; and when he saw him, he had compassion" (Luke 10:33, RSV). This parable takes its name *not* from the anonymous victim, but from the one who acts as the icon of divine Presence. The "good" Samaritan is in fact an outcast in the eyes of proper religious folk, yet becomes the mentor!

Only through some smarting Samaritan experience can one be admitted into this guild of wounded healers. Likewise, the nameless traveler's experience has now initiated him, along with any who admit their wounds, into an apprenticeship as journeyman: "Go and do likewise."

A practical example of this is illustrated in the old saw where a young manager asks a seasoned CEO, "What's the key to your decision making?" The mentor responds, "Good decisions come from experience, and experience comes from bad decisions." But we are not just talking about executing decisions, but about empowering compassion.

From my late twenties through my early forties, I set off from "Jerusalem to Jericho," ascending the ecclesiastical ladder with genuine but grandiose male energies. In midlife I met the angels on the descent, and got in touch with my impoverished male soul. Some of the anguish resulted from circumstances beyond my control, some from foolish notions of my own. But without these woundings I could not be an apprenticed Samaritan. (See chapter 7.) In the next chapter we will look at two forms of this male wound and the distancing it creates.

## PRAYER EXERCISE 5: Praying with the Samaritan

Find the text of the parable of the Good Samaritan in Luke 10:25-37. Take a few minutes for silent prayer. Then set the scene by visualizing the story. Will you create a back-then or a here-and-now setting? Allow the story to unfold, like an inner video. Let yourself identify with each of the characters: the man who sets out on a sure destination; the man after he is wounded; the attackers; the priest and Levite, not free to get involved (since touching blood would ruin their profession); the Samaritan, who himself has experienced rejection; the innkeeper-administrator. Finally, picture yourself as the student of the Law who came to Jesus with the questions, "Teacher, what must I do to inherit eternal life?" and "Who is my neighbor?" Continue the dialogue with Jesus, using a journal or a notebook. (See question 2 on page 46.)

OPTION: Groups can use Resource II, Scripture Sharing.

## PRAYER EXERCISE 6: Who Am I?

Try this exercise using your journal or notebook. You may do this in solitude, then share with another, or you may do the exercise in silence in a group session. At the top of the page, write, "Who am I?" Then prayerfully list all the external roles you can think of—for example: parent, child, your career role (engineer, musician, minister, sales rep, etc.), colleague, friend, golfer, pianist, woodworker. . . . Allow about five minutes for this. After each one, write, "God is merciful." Then write, "Who am I beneath the roles that people see?" Prayerfully, allow deeper images to emerge—for example: someone who appreciates beauty, loves

nature, is a lonesome cowboy, maker of music, seeker of God. . . .
Again after each one, write, "God is merciful." Allow another five
minutes. Notice differences between the two stages of this experience.

## For Personal Reflection or Group Conversation

1. "So the sin resulting from our foiled identity is not that men seek
power, but that we seek the wrong kind of power and from the
wrong sources." How does this connect with your own experience? With your experience of other men? In your work and family systems?

2. Spend some time reflecting on Prayer Exercise 5. To which characters in the story did you feel more drawn? In relation to them,
what stories or experiences from your life come to mind? (If you
are in a group or with a friend, spend some time listening to these
stories.)

3. Find a way to share something of your experience with Prayer
Exercise 6. What are some ways you can develop that will nurture
the deeper, more lasting images of your identity?

# RESTSTOP 1:
## Male Distancing

One result of the absent-father wound is that we pass it on in the form of distancing ourselves from other men who often yearn to be our friends—incidentally creating unrealistic expectations for intimacy from female relationships.

I was staying at Prince of Peace Abbey in Oceanside, California, where Kevin, a younger businessman and a Catholic, was also on retreat. At Sunday breakfast we were discussing worship, both remarking how much we enjoyed chanting the Psalms. Kevin complimented my singing: "You have a good voice."

"Oh, I just listen to the monks and then fill in the blank spaces." We laughed.

Next, he mentioned that I was the first person to welcome him on arrival two days earlier (he had asked me where to go to check in), and said, "Actually, I hope you won't be offended by this, but I thought you were a priest. It was something about your eyes."

I quipped, "Not many people ask me where to go, so when you asked me how to get to the office, it felt good to try it out!" He leaned back and we both had a macho laugh. Even in the moment I realized what I had done: I had used typical male humor to distance myself from my fear of intimacy with another man. (Of course, I also recognize that this kind of humor often functions as one form of male intimacy.)

On leaving the refectory, I paid attention to how empty I felt. Back in my room I was beginning to write this book on male spirituality, so I allowed myself to contemplate. In a few minutes I already knew what I wish I had done. When Kevin had given me a compliment, or maybe after cracking the joke, why had I not said, "Thank you"? Then I wondered, *What words or gestures might have occurred? Would we have reached out to each other?*

Later that morning as I made my way to the chapel for Sunday Eucharist, I was pondering how I would like to share these reflections with Kevin before he left—and just then he appeared! As we walked together, I was able to confess what I perceived had happened. We stopped and replayed the incident, repeating the above conversation. Then I looked at him and said, "Thank you." There was silence. Then I found myself saying, "It must be the priest in you that recognized the priest in me." And in that wonder-filled moment we hugged each other. (I now recall a similar phrase from Henri Nouwen.)

Fortunately the two of us were able to notice this incident of male distancing so it could be redeemed the very same morning, just before Kevin left the monastery at noon to attend his son's baseball game.

The trouble is that most of the time we do not even notice such incidents when another has tried to open his or her soul, let alone get the chance to replay a healing script so close to the time. Instead, we mask our lonely desire for intimacy in a myriad of ways that numb the male soul bit by bit, like a slow Novocain.

Most times we do not take the initiative, as Kevin did, even to affirm another guy on something as "feminine" as singing. Much less do we actually express physical affection to other men around us. If we continually distance ourselves and others from our true feelings, we become ready candidates for addictions, diseases, and burnout. And a lot of pain is suffered between the time of shutting someone out and when, if ever, we risk opening up the genuine, vulnerable self.

This microcosmic reconciliation with Kevin is a small sign for me, a harbinger of macrocosmic redemption that is possible in the estranged family, social, political, and environmental layers of the universe.

Fathers and children rarely acknowledge "the frightening spheres / between them, / a lonely distance / concealed in years / of dis-appointments: / "We'll get together then."

# Jacob and Esau

## Two Forms of the Male Wound

### Healing

I am not a mechanism, an assembly of various sections.
And it is not because the mechanism is working
       wrongly, that I am ill.
I am ill because of wounds to the soul, to the deep
       emotional self
and the wounds to the soul take a long, long, time,
       only time can help
and patience, and a certain difficult repentance
long, difficult repentance, realization of life's mistake,
       and the freeing of oneself
from the endless repetition of the mistake
which mankind at large has chosen to sanctify.

                —D. H. Lawrence

I recall as a child being mesmerized as my mother read the story of Jacob and Esau aloud from *Hurlbut's Story of the Bible*. But not till my fifties as I meditated on this scripture did I begin to see the personal connections with my youthful experience and that of my only sibling and older brother, David.

"Esau was a skillful hunter, a man of the field, while Jacob was a quiet man, living in tents. Isaac loved Esau, . . . but Rebekah loved Jacob" (Gen. 25:27-28). Esau and Jacob represent two forms of the experience of male wounding. The power of this ancient story continues to allow us to hear the voice of God speaking to us at multiple levels. On a social-historical level we hear echoes of warring antagonisms between the nomadic hunters and gatherers and the more domesticated shepherds and farmers.

On yet another level the story represents the psychological and spiritual journey of validating one's identity from external sources (Esau) vs. internal sources (Jacob). It is a classic paradigm of how human beings use their sibling rivalries, birth-order relationships, and family dysfunctions to sabotage and yet also, amazingly, to bless each other. And all this is under the providential umbrella of El-Shaddai, the greater Parent who will use these family shadows to bless the cosmos.

Here we see the ancient mythological archetypes of both the sins and gifts of masculine and feminine components of the soul: a blinded father who distances himself from his sons and an overly protective, manipulative mother both become the unwitting agents of a greater blessing.

Like Esau, from birth my brother seemed destined to follow the outward journey into sports and the agricultural world of my father, Francis David Winther Groff, whose name he bore. By contrast, I was named Kent for my maternal grandfather, a Presbyterian minister and graduate of Princeton Theological Seminary, from which I would later graduate. Through twin circumstances of childhood sickness and birth order, I would learn the art of collusion with my mother and the family doctor, a strange work of love that would cultivate my own journey inward. I could always talk my way into another few days of missing school because of croup and congestion. And even when I went back to school I would be carrying a note that said I had to stay inside for recess.

Jacoblike, I used my mother's overprotectiveness for all it was worth, to the detriment of athletic ability—and even swimming ability until it was required my freshman year of college. Yet my inside journey led to me to the world of art and music, designing and building, poetry and reading.

My method of getting what I wanted (though not necessarily what I needed!) was to win sympathy for my weaknesses, employ my verbal persuasive skills, and act the part of a nice guy. By contrast, my brother's way was by using strength, physical as well psychological—being aggressive and taking action.

## The Day of the Great Bulldozers: Action and Insight

I will never forget returning from school one day in late afternoon to the din of bulldozers on the north quadrant of our Chester County, Pennsylvania, farm. My father had taken a middle-of-the-road stance on progressive agricultural practices. He embraced the idea of contour strips, plowing the fields in "curves" and planting the rows horizontally, opposite to the natural flow of the water. But he had steadfastly resisted diversion terraces. This more modern method of conservation would create a continuous curved berm of land parallel to the contour strips to divert groundwater and thus conserve the water, soil, and minerals. But many acres would be planted with nothing but "waste" grass, too crooked and steep ever to be harvested. To my father this was unacceptable.

After months of trying in vain to persuade my father of the long-term value of these diversion terraces, my brother had used his name (the same as my father's, with good financial credit!) to engage an excavation company to bulldoze these long strips into terraces at a cost of several thousand dollars in 1950s currency.

That afternoon I watched as my father stood silently and helplessly, sniffing, his hands clasped, his face red with anger. My brother's action showed me a brand-new way to deal with my father's passivity.

On reading this, one of my children asked, "But what happened?" Of course the diversion terraces were a done deal. But what happened was a change in the constellation of family relationships. My brother had clearly established his identity as an agricultural entrepreneur, and as I look back on it, the community of other farmers affirmed my father for his son's ingenuity. For my part, it was a defining moment to confirm a form of action for me, too—my plan to leave the farm for college and probably for the profession of ministry, an action that would receive my father's blessing. My brother's gift that day was the gift of action; but I had begun to harvest my own gift and bring it to bear on the situation: the gift of insight, which in its own way now bears the fruit of action.

What happened on the day of the great bulldozers is still happening, as I have reflected on it, because my brother had begun to teach me a new dimension to humility. To claim one's gift and put it into action is to be willing to be humiliated; it is to place oneself vulnerably before others and risk being rejected, even wrong. (See Excursion 4.)

I am convinced that every man experiences some form of male wounding in relation to a father or a father figure. What that wounding experience is and the way the wound expresses itself in each unique life is varied: Jacob and Esau were in fact very different males. But if a wound is to be healed and embraced as a source of healing for others, it must first be noticed and named. Since diagnosis is the first step in healing, as I recount my experience, I hope that it will create connections that will help in the naming and healing process for you, the reader.

To what degree my Jacobness resulted from birth order, environment, or genetics, I will never know. I do know that being a latecomer is a significant factor. My mother was forty-two when I was born in 1942. She had suffered from rheumatic fever as a child and had a weak heart and constitution as an adult. This, coupled with possible genetic connection to my chronic childhood illnesses and allergies, predisposed my mother to be overprotective of the child she initially hoped would be a girl. (Kent, my mother's father, who died in 1936, had not been well much of his life, and anxiety and melancholia ran in my mother's family.) Her oft-expressed sentiment that "you're better than any daughter I could have" affected the issues of my male identity and the roles which I took on: doing home chores, cleaning and repairing the farmhouse windows, taking care of the grapevine and the cherry tree, landscaping and gardening.

It was David and my father who would go out to the fields, leaving Kent to do inside, home work. I was a professional at machine milking, even hand stripping, yet mine was inside barn work rather than my brother's external, field work of preparing hay and silage and cleaning out manure and fertilizing crops. All this he did using state-of-the art equipment if he could persuade my father to buy it.

## Silence and Sniffing: Experience of Male Absence

We were pretty clearly Jacob and Esau. Yet what still amazes me is that my father's response was the same to either of us any time we would challenge him. It was a kind of nonresponse accompanied by a sniff, at most a noncommittal comment, then silence, followed by a change of subject. He hoped, I believe, that by this means we would simply drop any threatening idea. My brother and I both knew, and confided to each other, that it would take two or three attempts to ever get my father merely to acquiesce to a request. To get a definite yes or no would happen if only one of us really pushed the cause, or if we joined together or got my mother involved.

In the biblical story, it is finally Jacob, with his mother's collusion, who receives the irrevocable blessing from the father at the very moment Esau is outdoors preparing to bring his offering to the father. By the time Esau appears with the offering, Isaac finds it necessary to reject it. I had always felt I had my father's blessing to leave the farm, go off to college, and enter some other kind of professional work. He used to tell me late at night that he hoped I would find a better life.

Thus, about the time of my sophomore year at Penn State University, I remember feeling very pained after learning that my brother had decided that he, too, wanted to attend Penn State in the college of agriculture, but that the answer had been no. My father, reporting through my mother, said David had not let them know ahead of time to prepare financially, as I had. My father's refusal to give my older brother the blessing of a college education was in a strange way crippling to me, since in some way my blessing was part of the cause, or the curse.

I knew, too, that just to get to the point of such a clear rejection instead of silence from our father must have meant there had been many attempts on my brother's part. No mention was made of a scholarship or loan, but I remember that one of my brother's responses was to begin decisively lobbying my father (and me) to make a creative father-son deal in which he could buy the farm for a reasonable figure, which in fact did happen within a few years.

Three years after my brother bought the farm from my father, he died traumatically at age thirty-one as a result of a broken leg from a tractor accident. After six weeks in the hospital, on his first full day at home, an embolism went to his lung before an ambulance could arrive, with my father again watching helplessly. My brother left a wife with three children, ages four, six, and eight, to experience a physically absent father.

Yet David died recognized as an leader in agriculture, church, and community. I will never completely understand the tragic, unconscious forces that colluded to snuff out the blessing of his life when outwardly he was so successful, but that's a longer story. Yet it illustrates the bankruptcy of subscribing to the journey as a straight line onward and upward.

## Nonresponse in the Family, beyond the Family

I have described my experience of my father's way of withdrawing when we needed him because it illustrates how two very different personality types (my brother and I) could experience the classic manifestations of the male wound of a distant father.

Mine was not a physically absent father. I was aware how some men traveled a lot, like dads of my "Du Pont" friends who had begun to move into our farm community after World War II, working in nearby Wilmington, Delaware. I am not sure which kind of absence is more wounding. But from the chapters of books and lives that have been opened to me, I am convinced that any man, even with the most devoted father, can trace his own male wound to an experience of a father's or father figure's physical or emotional absence.

A woman with Alzheimer's disease stuttered her frustration at her husband's lack of attentiveness. Looking right at me, she uttered one clear prophetic statement: "W-e-l-l, my husband's here but he's not here—if you know what I mean." I took it to heart. How many times I have been physically present, but not really "here" for my children, my spouse, a friend? In how many homes are those words echoed?

If you were to add together the men who have experienced a physically present but nonresponsive father, along with those with a physically absent father, that statistic would account for a vast majority of men's experiences. This male wound injures not only the well-being of our sons but also of our daughters—and of our entire society.

In *Sons of the Father*, Gordon Dalbey tells of a teenage girl who had finished getting ready for her very first date, to go out with a boy of whom her father actually approved. Yet as she proudly proceeded down the stairway, beautifully dressed, her father sat in a chair with a newspaper covering his face. She tried to get his attention. She tried again, verbally. But to no avail. She had to leave for that momentous event without her father's blessing. Later in her adult life, she was able to understand what had happened. The father had been so filled with fear of losing his daughter and being abandoned that he could not bring himself to acknowledge her.[1] Much overt male anger rises out of fear of abandonment, and fear is also the source of much of silent withdrawal even from those we desperately want to love.

Beyond one's family and friends, the nonresponsive "father figure" also inflicts pain on others in society when apprentices look for validation, but get none. The theme of "silences," so important in women's literature, shows how the nonresponse in a male-dominated world creates a painful, stifling rejection.

Willa Cather, before she was well known, had gotten the courage to write to her much-admired mentor, Henry James—sending him a copy of her book *The Troll Garden*. As Tillie Olsen tells in *Silences*, James never responded. Indirectly James wrote to a mutual friend belittling the young Cather's work as well as her being a female author, though he still promised the friend he would respond to Cather. He never did. The nonresponse, like my father's sniff, cast a long spell of writer's block and shame on this wonderfully talented author. Nearly a decade later, when the spell was broken by Sarah Orne Jewett, Cather would give the world the literary treasure, *O Pioneers!*—followed by a flood of other works.[2]

## A Wound That Can Become a Source of Healing

This is a good place to return to the Samaritan journey from Jerusalem to Jericho and the anonymous persons and processes at work in your life to "pour oil and wine" on the wound. When D. H. Lawrence said, "It is not because the mechanism is working wrongly, that I am ill. / I am ill because of wounds to the soul, to the deep emotional self," he meant that the "mistake" is precisely that: to think of oneself as a mechanism.

The necessary movement toward healing will be to engage in a cathartic cleansing of the grit of fear and the infection of anger that's gotten into this wound of the soul—which is what numbs the feeling function in a man.

## PRAYER EXERCISE 7: Notice the Male Wound— Being Loved

Begin with prayer in silence, asking for God's protection and healing. Reflect over your own life, and notice times when you experienced some absence or withdrawal of intimacy from a father or male figure. As you go to that experience, invite Jesus to enter a particular scene. See what gestures or words occur. Spend some time writing in your journal, then sharing with a spiritual friend.

OPTION: Each time you come to a difficult scene in your life, hear these words as if directly from God to you: "You are precious in my sight, / and honored, and I love you" (Isa. 43:4). Continue to repeat them frequently.

## PRAYER EXERCISE 8: Images for God

Begin with silent prayer. Ponder some feelings and associations that come to mind when you think of your biological or adoptive father, or father figures in your childhood family. Note some of the qualities in your journal. Consider how these affect your understanding of God. Now read the text of Isaiah 40:9-11, comparing the two images of God as a strong leader (v. 10) and as a nurturing shepherd (v. 11). (See the same two images in Deut. 1:30.) How are these two aspects related to your experience of "father"? Converse with God about your insights. Then, find a way to share your reflections with a friend or a group.

## For Personal Reflection or Group Conversation

1.  Can you relate the warring antagonisms between the nomadic hunters and gatherers and the more domesticated shepherds and farmers to the cultural history of the area of the country where you live? to the history of your congregation or local community? to systems within your own family?

2.  With whom do you identify more: Esau, oriented toward the external world of action, or Jacob, oriented more toward the internal world of reflection? How can each balance the other?

3.  What is your experience of the absent father (or father figure)—more physical absence or emotional absence? Can you see connections with your own relationships?

4.  How does the absent-father concept relate to your images of God as Father? How do you think women experience this? (See chapter 6, "Healing Images of God." See also Reststop 1.)

5.  "Jacob and Esau represent two forms of male wounding." What do you think? How does this play out for you?

# EXCURSION 3:
## Mentsh—and the Wounded Feeling Function

*J*ourney as a paradigm for male spiritual development would seem to fit hand in glove—but perhaps too much so, perpetuating the image of the medieval knight, so intent on his daring mission that he suppresses the pain of wounds in battle. Yet the tradition of the troubadour integrated feeling with task, singing with great passion for his beloved. Milan Kundera writes in *Immortality* about "the man who has learned to feel":

> *Homo sentimentalis* cannot be defined as a man with feelings (for we all have feelings) but a man who has raised feelings to a category of value. . . . The transformation of feelings into a value had already occurred in Europe some time around the twelfth century: the troubadours who sang with such great passion to their beloved.[3]

No one illustrates this better than Cervantes: Don Quixote is moved with compassion for Aldonza Lorenzo, who sees herself as nothing but a prostitute, a thing to be used to give sexual pleasure to men. Don Quixote sees into the beauty of her soul and names her Dulcinea. But it is his decision to assign value to his feelings that redeems Aldonza's life and shows his life to be a paradigm of the hero's journey which truly integrates gentleness and strength: a *mentsh* in Yiddish.

Robert Moore and Douglas Gillette have written about male sexuality and spirituality using the ancient motifs of *king, warrior, magician, and lover.* (See Excursion 5.) If ever we can see these four jarring archetypes of male experience integrated into a healthy unity it is in the life of this *Man of La Mancha*, Don Quixote. Using his intuitive wisdom and gentle strength to defend Aldonza, finally she is transformed and becomes an icon of empowering love.

Timeless myths and novels portray gentle strength born out of such abandonment. Victor Hugo's autobiographical experience lies at the heart of his character Quasimodo in *The Hunchback of Notre Dame* and the amazing hero-lover, Jean Valjean, in Hugo's classic *Les Miserables*.

And in Charles Dickens's *Great Expectations*, Pip, who was born penniless, receives an anonymous legacy to give him the best education in London schools. Yet, as a successful young adult, Pip shamelessly turns a poor man away from his door. Later Pip is transformed by the revelation that the stranger he rejected was in fact the selfless benefactor who had labored till he was skin and bones, the one to whom Pip owes his education and his life. *Great Expectations* is our story: the judgmental oppressor and the poor orphan are both parts of the self. And like Pip, by being ashamed of your "orphaned" feelings you may go through life beating up on part of your own psyche that has great potential—and you may unconsciously reject others who would help you.

"The poor live with less padding between them and the raw forces of life," Flannery O'Connor wrote in *Mystery and Manners*. Then she quoted Rudyard Kipling—that "if you wanted to write stories not to drive the poor from your doorstep."[4] All these writers have in common the ideal prototype of the integrated human being: a *mentsh*.

To cultivate ways to embrace the poor can be a key to inner healing for our desensitized feeling function. The poor make us uncomfortable because they remind us of the poor fallow furrows of our own psyches that are actually the raw materials of rich sentiment and gentle strength. The Bible, the ancient myths, the world's religions, and the great literature really have one and the same theme: that *homo sentimentalis* not only has feelings but can learn to pay attention to his feelings and assign them value, redeeming his experience. The result will change not only our outward relationships but will simultaneously deepen our own inward journey. By loving the poor, in some mysterious way, a man is loving the poor child and frightened beast in himself—and is paradoxically then in touch with the divine. It is the movement from a fragmented self to becoming a *mentsh*—a "congruent self."

# Men and Anger

## Nine Ways to Pray Our Emotions

> Apathy is frozen rage.
> —Mary, Chicago, 1969

> Hope has two beautiful daughters: their names are anger and
> courage. Anger that things are the way they are. Courage to
> make them the way they ought to be.
> —Saint Augustine

I will never forget the teaching of "Mary," who was brought from
the streets of Westside Chicago at the time of riots in the late sixties
to help teach us minister-types in a training program in urban ministry. "Apathy is frozen rage," she would say. Like a liturgical refrain,
during this month-long seminar whenever someone described another
incident of violence, we would hear it again, "Like I say, apathy's just
frozen rage."

A couple of months later I took a course called "The Psychology
of Education" at the University of Chicago from Allison Davis,
author of a classic series on descendants of slaves, *The Eighth
Generation*. (I recall my ecstasy when in 1993 he was honored with a
Dr. Allison Davis Black Heritage postage stamp!) The course could
be summarized by Davis's repeated phrase: "Depression is anger
turned inward." It sounded only slightly more scholarly and Freudian
than Mary's refrain; I was sure the two had colluded!

I know of no man who does not struggle with anger directly and indirectly. As in the story of *Beauty and the Beast*, maybe it is a monstrous fear of never being loved or of being abandoned that produces the outrage. Or maybe we experience just the opposite: feeling stuck or depressed as the result of buried anger.

## Tears and Anger: Two Gifted Cousins

Probably some frozen anger lay behind my father's inability to express his feelings and his withdrawal from my brother and me in moments of need. Despite this habit of distancing himself, my father gave me two wonderful nonverbal gifts: tears and tenderness. I recall being held on his lap and feeling his unshaven morning whiskers against my face. And it may seem odd, but I can recall incidents that would trigger his easy tears, and I would feel close to him. An aunt once made the hurtful remark to my mother that he was a crybaby. Explanations abounded.

When my wife met my father, she noticed his easy tearing. By the seventies, I had begun to associate it with his fresh grieving over my brother's early and tragic death along with the loss of the family farm which he could daily see from his window. But then I learned that stroke can predispose a person to cry easily, and he had experienced what appeared to be a few ministrokes. He finally died of a major stroke on March 12, 1983, exactly two months after my mother's death on January 12. I used to wish I had known the connection between stroke and tears when he was alive. Yet his tears predated any ministrokes.

What I did not want to admit to myself was a truth that I learned only in recent years from an addictions counselor: *When you see someone who cries easily, try to get the person to express anger; when you see someone who's easily angered, try to get the person to cry.*

When Augustine said, "Hope has two beautiful daughters: anger and courage," he expressed a transformative view of anger. One could also say, "Anger and tears are two gifted cousins."

## The Family Secret

I am sure my father's crying was related to painful emotions of grief. He told how in his teen years he lost his father from a heart attack, how he quit school to manage the family farm, and how he watched as two different barns were struck by lightning and burned. Having learned from helping his father rebuild the first, he rebuilt the second with help from a few neighbors in the wake of his father's death.

Then there was the unnamed ghost in his father's family closet which he never talked about, but which my mother and a favorite aunt decided to confide in us when we got to be teenagers. I remember my mother taking my brother and me aside to tell us one summer afternoon. This "ghost" had caused my then-Mennonite grandfather Clarence Daniel Groff to be shunned by his community near Honey Brook, Pennsylvania: He had first married Kate Wanner, then later fell in love with her younger sister—and he divorced Kate to marry Sallie Wanner, my own grandmother. Fleeing to Haddonfield, New Jersey, they were befriended by a Presbyterian layperson for whom my father was named—Francis David Winther. That is how my parents would later come to meet each other in a Presbyterian Church where my mother's father, Kent, was pastor. This family secret accounts for why I am a "congenital" Presbyterian!

My mother and my aunt were the true heroines in this story. None of the men in my father's generation ever spoke of this secret. Yet because my mother opened this chapter of our family system, as an adult I have also been able to reclaim treasures from my grandparents' Anabaptist heritage.

Knowing the story has helped me think differently of my father. Had my grandfather still been a Mennonite when the two barns burned, there would have been instant community barn raisings, instead of long, laborious rebuildings. Had this thought ever occurred to my father or my grandfather? There had to be deep, unspoken, unwept grief: "Give sorrow words. The grief that does not speak / Whispers the o'er-fraught heart and bids it break" (Shakespeare, *Macbeth*, IV.iii).

But just as this family pain was a source of my father's tears and tenderness, these have become his poor yet precious gift to me. Somewhere along the journey I began to notice that I, too, cry more easily than most men, and I noticed that I was always trying to explain away my father's tears, at the same time explaining away my own.

In a macho society where "big boys don't cry," anger is a legitimate male emotion, but never grief. I can remember the feeling in my stomach when television cameras captured Senator Edmund Muskie crying in public, ending his political career. As Robert Bly pointed out in an interview with Bill Moyers, Abraham Lincoln was the last national figure to validate grief as a politically correct and healthy emotion.

Now I have quit trying to analyze my father's tears—but why am I writing about them? Just as I write these words, I am reminded of a TV program that reported how chemical analysis demonstrated that tears from deep emotions are quite different from tears from a pinched finger in the car door. The bottom line is that tears of anguish give the body a necessary catharsis. I trust this as good, down-home, spiritual, psychological, and physiological wisdom. A good cry is a good thing, a catharsis for buried anger and grief.

So why do I write about my father's tears? I just want to notice his and my own, and pay attention to what they are telling me. For it is in paying attention to tears or any other common "drops of experience" (a rich phrase from the scientist-philosopher Alfred North Whitehead) that one can discover the greatest mystery of the cosmos!

The megamystery (Greek *mysteriōn*) that swallows up all our petty deadly family secrets is the mystery hidden for ages but now revealed in Jesus the crucified Messiah. This cosmic Mystery breaks down the dividing walls of hostility in family systems, church, or social institutions. (See Ephesians 2:14.) It is the messianic secret (*mysteriōn*) in the gospel parables: a mustard seed growing into a sheltering tree, a bit of yeast leavening the whole loaf, a hidden treasure in a field (Matt. 13:10-11, 31-33, 44).

Every man has within his life experience a hidden wholeness—as Thomas Merton named it, a metaphor of meaning, a healing hologram: this hidden seed, this secret leaven, this buried treasure, this mysterious pearl. But like the irritating grain of sand in the oyster, the place where it is buried is usually at the very point of anger, pain, and anguish.

As boys, we are taught that a wound is shameful, that to let a wound stop you from playing makes you a sissy. Yet Robert Bly's insight in *Iron John* embodies the radical gospel: "Our story gives a teaching diametrically opposite. It says that where a man's wound is, that is where one's genius will likely be. . . . That is precisely the place for which we will give our major gift to the community." While this especially applies to men, is it not true for everyone? Is this not the central meaning of Jesus' cross and resurrection? What is some life-in-death hologram that serves as a healing metaphor in your story-journey?

It was Jackie Robinson's mother painfully uprooting him from his abusive father and moving him to California that prepared him for his destiny as the first African American inducted into the Baseball Hall of Fame. It was Antoine de Saint-Exupéry's agony and anger in a for-saken New York apartment that gave birth to *The Little Prince*.

It was my brother and my father standing on the day of the great bulldozers, with me observing, that brought the gift of insight. It became a defining moment for me, a death-dealing yet life-giving para-ble of holy action emerging out of healing anger.

There is no wound without pain, and no pain without anger. And that anger, whether buried or exploded, is what we must learn to pay attention to and to pray if we are to offer the whole self to God.

## Nine Methods to Pray Our Anger

Unfortunately, prayer is often misused to deny anger. "You'd better go pray about that" usually translates as a recommendation to stuff your "bad" feelings rather than expressing them to God. Yet mindful-ness is the key spiritual principle in both Christianity and Judaism, all religions of East and West, tribal and universal. Prayer begins as awareness.

So whatever helps you notice some experience and the feelings it brings to the surface, offer that experience to God; and listen to any-thing God may want to say through it—that may rightly be called prayer.

I am not writing about male psychotherapy, but about male *spiri-tuality*. It is not just a description of the wound, but about how to offer it to God; not a diagnosis of the wound, but how to find a gift in it. As one beggar showing other beggars where to find bread, I offer nine methods that assist me to pay attention to my own anger: to notice it, offer it, then listen through it to God.

### 1. Praying the Psalms.

When I lead retreats, I open my Bible to the Psalms, mentioning that John Calvin said this prayerbook of the Bible contains "an anatomy of all the parts of the soul." I ask, "What are the moods of the soul that these pray-ers lift up to God?" Answers come back: joy, anger, beauty, suffering, peace, desolation, ecstasy, rage, hatred—and I often add exhaustion, exhilaration.

I know of no better continuing prescription for anger than to pray oneself through the Psalms sequentially. Pay special attention to portions that feel uncomfortable; these often reflect unresolved feelings within the self that you are a bit embarrassed to name and offer to God. Author Madeleine L'Engle once said that she prayed through the entire Psalter monthly, five psalms each day—the Benedictine practice of the Order of the Holy Cross, of which I am an associate. I recommend beginning by praying one psalm (or portion of one) daily until reaching the one-hundred-fiftieth, then starting with the first again.

The Psalms invite us to offer our raw emotions in uncensored language to God. Luther understood this kind of visceral praying. A retreatant was praying silently and heard a construction worker say, "Holy sh__!" Reflecting later with the group, we pondered: Could this expression mask a yearning for life's "waste" to become a source of wholeness and holiness? Could it represent an unconscious "prayer" that the lowest place in our life might be consecrated: "Holy humus!" For this is not just about venting: *It is about offering one's anger to God.* Only then can negative emotions be relinquished to the Ground of our Being and become humus to nurture another thing of beauty. The Psalms invite us to do our own creative, psalmlike praying.

2. Using a journal to write or "art" your own psalm.

Try using a journal to paraphrase a "negative" psalm that mirrors feelings you are experiencing, using your own words or artwork. (Try doing this with Psalm 13, 54, or 77:1-10.) Or notice an experience of anger or joy (past or present), then ask, "God, what are you trying to say to me through this?"

Or, simply journal your feelings, then put "God" in front and "amen" at the end, and you have written your own Psalm! Sometimes you can "write your way home." But writing by itself may not work. So I suggest "cluster journaling." Put a word or image that's on your mind in the middle of a page, then create a "cluster" of words around and below it like a spider-web—writing in a free-flow association whatever words or images occur to you. Then below the whole thing, try writing a psalmlike prayer with words. Here's a simple example of cluster journaling using an ordinary experience:

WORD OR IMAGE
(example: stiff neck)

WRITTEN PRAYER:
(using phrases or theme from cluster journaling, above)

A Lakota Christian came to his pastor saying he was unable to pray. He had been set up by undercover agents. It meant that he would serve time in jail and his land could be confiscated. The pastor recommended cluster journaling—suggesting that he incorporate this with his Native tradition of praying at sunrise and sunset. By beginning with an image and free-flow associations, he was able to give voice to his feelings—he could actually pray by writing his own psalm.

3. Using an image of nature to express anger.

A friend introduced me to this idea from Flora Slosson Wuellner in *Heart of Healing, Heart of Light*, and I invited the friend to try it out right on the spot. We sat for some minutes in silence. She then reported seeing her anger as the wave of the sea, rising to a crescendo and crashing . . . luring her feelings into the sea of God's love. In the same moment, I had pictured my anger as a bolt of lightning, zooming red-hot feelings into the cosmos to the heart of God.

4. Praying your emotions with your body.

The phrase "muscular Christianity" was popular during the early period of the YMCA (Young Men's Christian Association) movement. Praying with the body does not mean you have to think sports. I quip how "I'm athletically declined," related to my childhood illnesses. But now I have discovered I enjoy noncompetitive forms of exercise. I incorporate into my morning prayer a blend of tai chi movements with a Native American tradition of facing the four directions, praying for people to the East, South, West, and North—creating the pattern of the cross with my feet. And I do physical exercises for my back in rhythm to each phrase of the Lord's Prayer, and other exercises as intercessions for particular friends.

Try dedicating an activity for some person or cause: a racquetball game for a situation where someone constantly spars with you; gardening as a prayer for God to work up the soil of your soul. There are hundreds of ways to pray with the body, including a healthy incorporation of sexuality as a way to "present your bodies . . . holy and acceptable to God, which is your spiritual worship" (Rom. 12:1; see chapter 8). Walking connects with the biblical meaning of the spiritual life as our walk with God. Simple, centering prayer exercises to attend to our breathing provide a basic bodily way to cultivate an active life of prayer and contemplation. Certainly such kinesthetic prayer is a valuable way to cultivate attentiveness! (See chapter 12.)

### 5. Talking out your emotions.

Interpersonal prayer is a key to grief therapy: talk it out. When I meet with someone, I may observe, "So you've been praying the Psalms, you've prayed in your journal—but have you prayed by talking it out with your bishop, or your supervisor, or your spouse?" Also, talk it out with a spiritual companion, a safe person outside your own system of church, family, or business. Research shows benefits for cancer patients who "pray the stress" by talking it out with a support group, a Twelve-Step group, one-on-one with a spiritual director or counselor, or alone with God. "It is not good for the human being to be alone" (Gen. 2:18, AT). "Give sorrow words." Just hearing his own words can help a man break the emotional barrier and cry his pain to God or to another.

### 6. Praying with music and poetry.

Earlier I spoke about the Scottish man who would never be caught saying "I love you" to his wife, but she had learned to ask him to sing to her; she knew he could sing his feelings when he could not speak them. It is the same with God: Music and poetry (your own or others') become wonderful means of expressing oneself in prayer.

### 7. Practicing silent prayer and meditation.

Growing up among the Quakers in Chester County, Pennsylvania, I realize that merely the attitude of learning from silence became a part of who I am. Try repeating a centering phrase or word—one like *manna, agape, peace, Jesus, amor*—or *Maranatha*, "Our Lord, come!" (1 Cor. 16:22) Or simply center on a metaphor, an object, or a sound, feeling in your heart the love God has for you instead of hearing the distractions of the mind. Try taking longer periods for silence, such as an overnight retreat in a monastery or retreat center. Silence is one of the richest treasures of intrapersonal prayer.

8. Praying the stressors by reading.

I put this one next to last, because reading, which is usually more left-brain and cognitive, can easily sidetrack us from the more affective methods and keep us in our heads. But this depends on one's personality type, and what kind of book he uses. Reading can be therapeutic. A Presbyterian minister and author, who today is alive and well, discovered back in 1983 that he had acute leukemia. When visiting this friend in the hospital, I would observe stacks of books next to his bed. Reading about the disease became one of his primary ways of offering the experience to God. Reading a book on anger can be a way to "pray the anger," noticing the insights and offering the feelings to God. Most of our reading is *informational* (factual), but the ancient *lectio divina* or "prayerful reading" is *formational* (meditative). It is a good method for meditating with scripture, but also with any kind of reading. Short stories (I like Flannery O'Connor), mysteries, and novels can create healthful, prayerful ways of knowing oneself. *Stories* simultaneously stimulate activity in both right brain, creating images, feelings, senses, *and* left brain, using linear, sequential data.

9. Transforming anger into a cause.

This is the true meaning of *sublimation*—which differs radically from *suppression*. Suppression means stuffing your feelings, unconsciously. Creative sublimation is a process of being very much aware of the feelings related to the original anger or problem, but intentionally following a course of action whereby the feelings are channeled into a positive cause. MADD (Mothers Against Drunk Driving) was founded by families of victims of car crashes who now work for positive changes in highway safety. Mohandas Gandhi and Martin Luther King, Jr. understood well the art of sublimation.

Actually all these are part of a process of creative sublimation, which is finally not something *we* do at all, but a transformation the Spirit works in us. By practicing continual, repeated habits of noticing our emotions and offering them to God, we can claim the reality of Augustine's wisdom: that hope has two beautiful daughters, anger and courage.

## PRAYER EXERCISE 9: Praying Your Emotions

Focus on some area of stress or anger in your life. Prayerfully reflect on the above methods, and select one or two methods that you feel drawn to try—either once, or over a continuing period of time. For example, if you do not presently pray with your body, consider how you might incorporate some body prayer exercises into your daily period of prayer. Or try a method as one-time experience—such as letting your anger take the form of some aspect of nature.

## For Personal Reflection or Group Conversation

1.  What are the greatest barriers to healthy expression of anger?

2.  What differences do you notice between the ways men and women deal with anger?

3.  Ponder Saint Augustine's words on page 59. What do they say to you?

4.  Ponder your life to see if you can find an example of anger being used in a positive way. What enables transformation? (Find another person and converse about this.)

## RESTSTOP 2:
## Overextending, Being Stuck

A pastor in his forties consistently complained of feeling stuck. He would try new patterns for prayer and self-care, then lapse into distractions. Once as we met he recalled a time in adolescence when his parents had gone to choir practice. Alone and lethargic, in spite of homework that needed to be done, he entered his parents' bedroom where they had moved the TV. There he lay on their bed for a couple of hours, intermittently glued to the screen and beating on the bed out of frustration, knowing that his homework was not getting done. (I invited him to close his eyes and go back to that scene, to experience the feelings again, then after a time, to picture Jesus entering that room, to notice any gesture, any word that Jesus might say.) "Stuckness" was his unique sin and this was a specific prototype experience that helped us understand the general pattern.

But the way my friend's story connected with my own illustrates the principle of "the healer being healed." As I left to drive to a meeting with my own spiritual director, at a stoplight I pondered: *Is there a prototype experience of my unique sin?* In that instant, I recalled sitting at the dining room table of the family farmhouse late at night, filling out my application for Penn State University. Where it asked for strengths and weaknesses, I had turned to my mother and queried, "Do I have any weaknesses?" There it was, and is—this youthful messianic idealism, made just as clear in my mother's response, "Why of course, it's that you take on too many things at once!" I reflected on all this with my spiritual director.

Later in my own solitude I spent time doing the same meditation for myself as I had done with the pastor who met with me. I sketched the scene in my journal, with crayons, then wrote out a litany, dialoguing with Jesus. I said to Jesus, "This is my table." (The same table used for family celebrations was also the workspace where I did my homework, filled out forms and artwork to register each of the Holstein-Friesian cows, and completed applications for youth awards and college admission.) Then I heard Jesus say to me, "This is my table"—the table where your male wound is lifted up like the bread and wine of communion can now be a source of your gift to the community. The table of my work and celebration had become one.

Now each morning, on my hands and knees, I arch my back to a "table" position in a yogalike prayer exercise. I visualize Jesus saying to me, "This is my table." And I respond, "This is my table." Then I hear Jesus say, "Come as a child." I collapse into a fetal position on the floor and respond, "I come as a child." And I hear the words of Isaac Watts's hymn "My Shepherd Will Supply My Need," paraphrasing Psalm 23:

There would I find a settled rest, / While others go and come;
No more a stranger or a guest, / But like a child at home.

Months later, as I revisit these stories, I realize that my friend's experience of stuckness and mine of overextending myself represent two classic expressions of the male wound: the passive sin of paralysis and the dominative sin of idealism. In reality, all of us experience each of these sins to a greater or lesser degree, and at various stages of our lives. I too am often stuck, frequently after taking on too many ideas and projects. Jesus the Messiah offers healing for this awful splitting and flipping back and forth: the model of Jesus' rhythm of healthy passiveness and healthy assertiveness provides a healing prototype for the male soul.

# 6

# Healing the Male Soul
## Nine Ways to Pour on Oil and Wine

Several years ago I visited a halfway house in Western Ontario. . . . But a beautifully framed sign over the fireplace is the thing I remember best. It said, "Do you want to be right or well?". . . . It's hard to believe that there is any connection between the ability to "be wrong" and admit mistakes, and our physical or emotional health, but this age-old insight is being rediscovered in our time.

—Bruce Larson, *There's a Lot More to Health
Than Not Being Sick*

My father's form of distancing himself made it all the more possible for my mother's overprotection to fill the vacuum. Some of my elementary school teachers noticed this protectiveness and questioned my excessive absences. Yet amazingly enough, these dysfunctional dynamics that made me more like the Jacob indoors than the Esau outdoors created an opening for grace in my life. Through frequent respites in the innkeeper's caretaking (my mother's), I would embark on a different kind of journey on my way from Jerusalem to Jericho: an inward pilgrimage into the worlds of art, music, literature, and spirituality—making creative use of downtime.

The wound began to create its own healing. As an adult I have also begun to see my mother as the Great Permission Giver. She permitted my brother and me to learn of my father's family secret. She gave us political permission, telling us that for her mother "the sun rose and set on Woodrow Wilson," a Democrat! And the day my father's mother was taken to a nursing home, she gave us a true gift of permission: If someday she needed more care than we could give, she told us that she wanted us to take her to a home that could meet her needs. It was a gift that was later fulfilled.

And amazingly, too, I can say in so many ways now that my father's passive silences served as a mirror for me to better define what it was that I *needed* instead of only what I *wanted*. And I can say that out of his habit of steeling himself and masking his feelings, he taught me nonverbal ways of communicating. He himself was a master at nonverbal communication. He always had my brother and me stumped as to how he could "sniff" out whether some new neighbor he had never met was a Republican or Democrat, without ever asking directly!

So it is not really important that my father never finished high school (he took over the family farm when his father died), that in his life he never saw a psychiatrist—or that I have seen one for so many years to make up for it! It is not really important to figure out why he distanced himself in my times of need, or if his easy tears were triggered by genetics, ministrokes, sad experiences, buried emotions, or all of these. Too much analysis leads to paralysis.

I tell myself, what matters is that as often as I am aware of past dynamics in my life *now*, that I notice my feelings and offer them to God *now*—that I listen to God's invitation *now*. I need to trust God in this very moment, redeeming those very moments.

And this is the subject at hand: the movement from noticing the wounds and offering them to God—to experiencing healing at the hands of some surprise Samaritan, or some smarting experience. One of the greatest barriers to our own healing is that we may resist the "Samaritan" source of it. We would prefer the healing be mediated through the neat, clean hands of tradition.

## Healing vs. Curing: Spiritual Health and Male-Biased Culture

Perhaps out of my childhood physical illness and ongoing battles with allergies and manic-depressive tendencies, I have always been interested in spiritual healing and in "complementary medicine," that is, using forms of ancient natural medicine and spiritual healing to complement

Western medical technology. But I have also been equally suspicious of miraculous "curing" in what seemed a magical way that denied the reality of illness or created unhealthy expectations. I have seen too many persons blame self or God if they were not cured in a tangible sense.

But how is this theme of healing uniquely related to male spirituality? Medicine as it is generally practiced in Western culture reflects an overemphasis on two streams of male-dominative culture. And by default the complexities of cost and technology make it more akin to the lifestyle of the "expressway" than to that of the "road."

First, the emphasis is on the analytical and rational, which is actually a recent development since the Enlightenment. While medical science recognizes that dis-ease in a human being has a high degree of connection to the less quantifiable, affective components of life, our complex systems allow little time for these aspects. (See Excursion 6.)

Second, the language of Western medicine reflects another masculine bias in its primarily linear and external model of curing. People have heart *attacks* (as if invaded from outside), and surgery (invasive removal of an enemy) serves as the de facto medical model in the minds of many average people.[1]

Complementary (or alternative) medicine pays more attention to the body's own internal tendency to heal itself. Dr. Albert Schweitzer, who chose to leave the "good life" in Europe to serve in French Equatorial Africa, modeled this integration in his own life: He was simultaneously a physician and New Testament theologian, a musician and writer, a missionary and philanthropist. Schweitzer spoke of the will to live and of working with "the doctor who resides within each patient." That is the assumption of the nine forms that follow. Complementary medicine also addresses the underlying issues that aggravate personal and corporate illnesses: our dominative, task-oriented family and social systems. In this we need to follow the pattern of the Master Physician and Prophet.

## Nine Forms of Experiencing Healing

In each of these nine forms I am suggesting a double meaning; for example, "healing relationships" conveys not only *the healing of dysfunctional relationships* but also *positive relationships that heal*. In this way they provide a framework for complementary medicine—eliminating specific diseases, while also generating holistic health. While focusing on healing the male soul, these nine are adaptable to women as well.

## 1. Healing memories.

We need healing *of* negative memories, some so painful and long-buried that they can be recalled only in the presence of a trained therapist or spiritual director. But just as desperately we need to recall healing memories—memories that have the capacity to heal and hallow our lives, even retroactively. The practice of recalling what Frederick Buechner calls "moments of crazy, holy grace" can actually generate a healing for painful memories. (In my book *Active Spirituality* I have created a prayer exercise for this using Psalm 77:11-12.) No special training is necessary. Anyone can sit, be still, and recollect incidents of divine Presence. And there's great value in sharing such experiences.

## 2. Healing self-images.

Every human being is infected with negative self-images that need healing. To truly listen to the words of Isaiah 43:4—"You are precious in my sight, and honored, and I love you"—is at once very dignifying and humbling. The mathematician and mystic Blaise Pascal expressed repeatedly in his *Pensées* that there was nothing more important for a human being than to know one's baseness and one's humility, *and* to know one's greatness and one's dignity.

Just as we all have the need for healing of negative self images (I had a childhood friend, Leo, who was actually called "Stinky" by his family!), we know the healing power of life-giving self-images. A healing self-image for me is one of a photographic darkroom where the negative is developed in the light to create a positive print.

In working on this book, I hit the familiar impasse of feeling it was garbage: the project was impossible. I told myself (heard the Spirit whisper), "You know your best insights come out of the abyss, an empty space." I have learned to embrace that part of myself, so I was able to ride the monster of self-doubt down into the deep—break the sound barrier and write. Truly to know the self is to know God, and to truly know God is to know oneself, as John Calvin, Søren Kierkegaard, and a myriad of mystics have said.

3. Healing images of God.

We need healing *of* dysfunctional images of God, as well as affirming, healing images. A middle-aged woman was referred to me for spiritual direction. This woman, who had been in psychotherapy for over two decades, never saw the man who got her mother pregnant, and grew up with a shamed mother and a stepfather who abused her. She said it was impossible to believe in God with all the male images in the Bible. Jesus was male, too, so I shouldn't push that, she said.

Another time I recall meeting with a young man who had told me he had been abused as a child. I gave him Isaiah 49:15 for his meditation:

> Can a woman forget her nursing child,
>     or show no compassion on the child of her womb?
> Even these may forget,
>     yet I will not forget you.

This suggests an image of God as mother. "But," he later confronted me, "my *mother* was the one who abused me."

Each story illustrates how individual experience colors any words or images of the Divine. Our metaphors for God lead us to the place on the horizon *beyond which is God*. This is what the medieval mystic Meister Eckhart meant when he spoke in terms of "the God beyond God"—the One hidden beyond our distorted images of God. One of the benefits of disciplining myself to use inclusive language in my writing and prayers has been to discover so many positive images of God that I had paid little attention to: God as a rock that gives birth; a river, a tree of life; a sun and a shield; a shelter and a fortress; fire and light; friend and savior; a mother eagle bearing us on her wings. The amazing thing is that in addressing God as *Abba*, Jesus imbues the traditional image of Father with radically intimate qualities, as Roberta C. Bondi has written in *Memories of God*. As mentioned earlier, God is strong yet compassionate, like C. S. Lewis's image of Aslan the Lion.

4. Healing perceptions.

Sometimes we need healing of a mistaken perception that causes pain. A grandfather felt a bit slighted that his son's baby boy was not given his own name even as a middle name, but rather named for its maternal grandfather. Sometime later, his daughter-in-law told him, "You know, in Jewish tradition it's an honor to carry on a deceased person's name, but it would be an insult to name a child for someone who's still living." Such healings of perception can also transform resentment or self-doubt. A worker may be told he was let go because of downsizing, yet is never allowed to know the real reason (company politics). People suffer for years from misperceptions. That is why we need healing of our social systems.

A positive perception has power to hallow your life and counter negative perceptions. A dream may be the bearer of such a healing perception. In the late eighties a neighbor told me I should cut down a bothersome crab apple tree beside our cottage at Chautauqua, New York. A bit annoyed, nevertheless I made plans to have it cut down. That winter I had a dream: *Planted beneath the crab apple tree was a seedling maple. Then suddenly folks were celebrating Christmas out in front of our cottage!* When I returned the next spring, there it was—a tiny maple I had never noticed, now shading the study where I am writing this. The dream is a vocational parable: I had just resigned from a large church when "crabby" conflict cut off two decades of ministry to congregations. Yet beneath this conflicted ministry, a seedling call to deepen my own spiritual life had developed into Christmas: giving birth to my writing and teaching and a fledgling nonprofit corporation, Oasis Ministries for Spiritual Development. The healing perspective of this dream still energizes me.

5. Healing anger.

Christiane Northrup, M.D., who teaches at University of Vermont College of Medicine, says suppressed anger is a major factor in heart disease, cancer, and other illnesses.[2] It is at the heart of the crisis of spirituality and sexuality. Much of our unresolved hostility results from male fear of intimacy. We use culturally acceptable anger to mask our unacceptable loneliness, causing pain to our own soul and others.

This is why the Psalms are so valuable. They give permission to express our deepest angst—a word that combines anger and loneliness. Pray the Psalms, write your own psalm, journal, pray with nature, work it out in physical exercise, meditate on it, talk it out with another, and talk it out with God. Follow the Twelve Steps of Bill W. and Dr. Bob: Forgive an enemy, make restitution. And where it is not possible, offer the anger to God as your poor gift to be used for a greater cause. We cannot ignore this healing potential in anger. In genuine sublimation, holy anger heals and hallows, giving purpose to one's whole life.

6. Healing purpose.

Seneca said, "Without knowing which port one is sailing toward, there is no such thing as a favorable wind" (AT). To be well, the body, which includes our brain and nerve cells, needs a purpose to live for! We need to discover a cause in life that fires our passion to work for com-passion, something beyond ourselves for which to live and die. John Biersdorf's book, *The Healing of Purpose*, accents this need for healing when one's outer work is dissonant with one's inner values. Victor Frankl, a psychiatrist imprisoned by the Nazis, gave himself to the cause of studying why some persons with the same disease and frostbite lived while others died. In *Man's Search for Meaning*, Frankl concluded: *The person with a why to live can survive almost any how.*

To recollect ordinary incidents of spiritual awareness can serve as a *hologram of meaning* for one's life. The dream of the underplanted maple is one such example for me. Like the poet Blake you can "see the world in a grain of sand" in such experiences if you pay attention.

Living life on purpose releases positive neurotransmitters into the bloodstream. "The Lord will fulfill the divine purpose for me" (Ps. 138:8, AT). "It would be well, and proper, and obedient, and pure, to grasp your one necessity and not let it go, to dangle from it limp wherever it takes you. Then even death, where you're going no matter how you live, cannot you part," writes Annie Dillard in *Teaching a Stone to Talk*. Even retroactively, a personal mission statement can help things come together and flood your whole life with meaning. (See page 138.)

7. Healing relationships.

A male-female pastoral team on a church staff felt helpless as a mother of small children lay dying of cancer, estranged from her father. As a way of praying with her, the woman pastor asked if there was anything she wanted to talk about, offering to take notes. The dying woman whispered a story of childhood abuse by her father, which she had never told. Later, after the dying woman chose to share these notes with her siblings, they all requested the male pastor to deliver this "letter" to her father. This was very risky; things could blow up. Even the patient's mother had misgivings about the plan. Nevertheless the letter was delivered. What happened the next day the pastors describe as a miracle! The father had asked to be reconciled, and the daughter invited him in to be a caretaker—much welcomed by the family—for the final days of her life. The healing of relationships can be the healing even though the body dies.

And there's the double meaning: We need to place ourselves intentionally in the context of *healing relationships*. Sometimes a person has no choice but to remain in a toxic family or work situation; other times one must extract oneself from great pain. Either way, it is lifegiving to place oneself in relationships that generate catharsis and healing.

### 8. Healing bodies.

I was presenting these ideas to a group training to be spiritual directors, among them Greg, a successful businessman in his thirties, who only eight months earlier had been facing end-stage leukemia. But now physicians at Johns Hopkins Hospital have given him permission to use the "R" word to describe his amazing remission. Since I had placed healing of the body next to last on this list, I wondered how Greg would respond. I turned to him and said, "You're the only one qualified to talk about the healing of the body."

Greg's response was overwhelming. Speaking also as a recovering alcoholic, he told us that healing of the body had become unimportant. What mattered to him most was the healing of relationships, with God and self and others, of his purpose for living, of his anger, of his outlook. And a big part of staying whole, he said, is the need to become a "wounded healer" for someone else by telling your story.

What matters, we all concluded, is to allow the human temple of the Holy Spirit to regenerate its own healing powers, *to live in this present moment with purpose and meaning.*

### 9. Healing social systems and environment.

One thing that still bothers me about some "spiritual" healing services is the privatized nature of much of it. Healing means promoting health, and it certainly includes working on social causes that foster the healing of the environment: air, oceans, trees, wetlands, deserts, wildlife. Sadly, most Western institutions—educational, medical, military, government, business, even religious—are programmed for an "expressway" mode of life: fast-track achievement and bottom-line, measurable productivity, which contribute to diseases in our bodies.

So healing the soul has implications for social systems. Our political institutions also have potential to generate social healing or destructive violence. Walter Bruggemann in *The Powers* talks about institutional healing and the power of a curative ethos in social institutions. In *Stretch Out Your Hand: Exploring Healing Prayer*, Robert D. Webber and Tilda Norberg illustrate the healing of social systems, describing a corporate exorcism for apartheid in South Africa and a representative healing service for a conflicted church.

The ability to feel what it is like to be a minority in some aspect in one's own life can open up new worlds for empathic change. As you read this, pause. Recall a couple of specific examples where you have personally been a victim of institutional bias.

*Attitudes of the leaders of any institution make a powerful difference in effecting institutional healing.* What if public and private institutions "baptized" *relationship* as equally valid as *productivity*? What would it mean if we institutionalized time-outs and skills for reflection on experience? What if, at a very minimum, employees were given company incentives to explore poetry, keep a journal, participate in a human relations growth group, say, for half an hour a week? There are models. Poet David Whyte has found corporations willing to try the approach of allowing the reflective side of human experience to become integral to the activity of business. (See his book *The Heart Aroused*.)

## Healing through Failure: An Institutional Example

This kind of redeeming reflection can happen on an institutional level, though it may not seem like traditional success. In *The Active Life*, Parker J. Palmer tells of being asked to consult with a suburban church which had entered into a partner relationship with a church in an inner-city area. The suburban church members had experienced nothing but frustration. They felt their efforts to relate to the other church were not working, even though they had tried to work on mutual goals and avoid paternalism. During the course of the meeting, the insight began to dawn on the group that this very experience of powerlessness might be as close as these privileged Anglo-Saxon folks could ever get to the daily feelings of frustration and helplessness their sisters and brothers in the city congregation experienced. In a reverse kind of way, this spiritual impasse became the beginning of institutional healing and corporate interior learning.

Healing for the privileged suburban church was mediated through their strange feeling of rejection via a biblical "corporate" Samaritan, in trying to establish a partnership with an inner-city church they were trying to help.

For journeymen apprenticed by the Master Physician and Prophet, who healed individuals but also challenged the systems that crippled people, the question is, What would Jesus be doing? "Go and do likewise" is the continuing process of mentoring. To that we now turn.

## PRAYER EXERCISE 10: For Healing a Relationship

Meditate on a relationship where you feel some strain, with an adult son or daughter, a colleague, a friend of the past or present. Spend at least ten minutes visualizing the person alone, and then at some point, picture the person with you in some context. Return to picturing the person alone—surrounded with light. Hold the person in the light, without words, desiring God's best, God's peace. Conclude by saying the Serenity Prayer, once for yourself, then a second time for the other person. Ponder whether you might call, write, or visit the person you have prayed for to listen, to offer a simple "I'm sorry," to say you wish the relationship could have been better—or to ask forgiveness or extend forgiveness. If such a meeting is not possible, write in your journal what you would like to say, as a prayer: "Holy, loving God, receive these concerns that I am expressing here for (name)." NOTE: If you are a father of a young adult, consider finding an appropriate time to say simply, "(Name), I wish I could have done a better job of being a father (could have spent more time together, telling you more about myself, etc.)" Wait, prayerfully, for a response.

## For Personal Reflection or Group Conversation

1. Reflect on the twofold meaning in each of these nine areas, for example, healing of negative memories and positive memories that heal. In your experience, which is more difficult, or more important?

2. With the changing medical context, increasing technology, and more outpatient surgery, how would you apply these ideas to the life of your local church? What are some of the values and risks for a local church in offering a service of wholeness?

3. Dr. Victor Frankl wrote, "The person with a why to live can survive almost any how." How is this related to the healing of purpose?

4. "One of the greatest barriers to our own healing is that we may resist the 'Samaritan' source of it." How might cross-cultural experiences and friendships be agents of healing? What happens if you apply this to Twelve-Step programs? To programs of the local church?

5. How does male-biased culture affect our models of medical care?

6. What are the differences between curing and healing?

# EXCURSION 4:
# The Imitation of Christ—A New Look at Humility

The problem with much traditional talk of humility is that it smothers us with a form of self-denial that runs counter to the Jesus of the Gospels, and which turns thoughtful people away from Christ. It can make the Good News into the bad news of human perfectionism. It can also turn spiritual apprentice-mentor relationship into a demonic form of control by the mentor. Besides, no martyr ever set out to suffer.

Humility, in a strange way, is actually spiritual self-confidence: confidence that you can celebrate and delight in the gifts of others while at the same time claiming your own. So it is a God-confidence, a trust born of God in the economy of the Spirit that there are enough gifts to go around. Both your neighbor and you can claim your potential for the good of the cosmos, without exploiting each other. This is genuine humility: to risk putting your unique gifts on the firing line.

It is a trust in the One whose nature is to create abundance out of scarcity, as you place your life—like the meager loaves and fishes—in the hands of the Christ before the thousands who hunger (Mark 6:30-44). You must be willing first of all to believe that you have value in the eyes of One who chooses to take you and bless you: "You are my beloved child." Then you must believe that the very brokenness itself—of your life and of the world—when placed in the hands of this Messiah, can become the source of blessing, painfully dividing in order to multiply the scarce treasure out into the world of human need.

Such daring God-confidence will also celebrate your neighbor's original blessing. You will rejoice when his or her brokenness is transformed into gifts that multiply even more than your own. It is the new form that humility must take in our time. In this global village, we cannot afford a private humility. Rather than try to beat ourselves into shape, we are called to cultivate a humility on behalf of others, to distribute the gifts of the cosmic Christ for the good of the world. It is a new look at the imitation of the Christ. Christ is the model of empowering love: "For God did not give us a timid spirit, but rather a spirit of power, and of love, and of sound thinking" (2 Tim. 1:7, AT).

What would Jesus do? has become a popular slogan. But the focus is on the wrong thing, on the *do*. It needs to be translated, What would Jesus *be* doing? What would Jesus *be*? Presence, power, peace: Any lasting action in the world needs to come from the deep center of wholeness, or it will be so much chaff. Jesus modeled this by a continual pattern of retreat and involvement, solitude and community.

What would Jesus be *doing*? What Jesus would be about would flow from who he is. And he would be about loving, listening, learning, laughing—and leaving us to continue what he began to do and teach (Acts 1:1). That is what we need to be about, so that when we leave we will have empowered others not just to do something, but to be the presence of Christ.

That brings us back to having the courageous humility to submit our gifts to the community, as when I dare to submit a manuscript—risking rejection. It is to take up the cross, not lie down like doormats; to take up the cause of narrowing the frightening gap between the rich and the poor, to live on behalf of the least of these; to befriend the fearful, marginalized part of your own soul that may be too timid to speak up. "Take my yoke upon you, and learn from me" (Matt. 11:29).

The imitation of Christ is not mimicking external actions of Jesus, but becoming by your baptism who Jesus is: a unique incarnation of God's love. You are empowered in order to serve with energy, intelligence, imagination, and love. And genuine humility means yearning to see your neighbor empowered with these same gifts.

# 7

# Apprentices, Journeymen, and Mentors

Youth, apprentices, and mentors
Help us learn this craft of faith—
In a guild that spans the centuries, eons,
Leaving footprints on the path.

*—Guide Us All On This Day Journey*

I had enlisted my twenty-four-year-old son to help me learn the complexities of my new computer. Sitting next to me, he noticed the worry and impatience in my voice, and I realized there was a lot more going on than my anxiety about a computer. I heard his crisp words: "Just relax. Don't panic, Dad; one thing at a time." I had a flashback: Instantly I saw myself, as clearly as if it were yesterday, next to my son on the front seat of my car, saying those same words to him as he clutched, shifted, and braked, anxiously learning to operate a stick-shift transmission just as his two older sisters had done before him.

Could this moment of frustration become a moment of intimacy? I paused, recalling my own father's way of withdrawing in such tense moments. Now in my fifties, could I discover a new dimension to this craft of fathering? I found myself telling my son of the flashback going on in my head. We laughed and embraced. Then we proceeded with the task.

How quickly the apprentice-mentor role reverses itself! This story is repeated a thousand different ways. You have children or you know younger colleagues who are wiser than you in a myriad of different fields. Sadly, incidents when the elder feels dumb often end in shaming each other. The spiritual invitation in such occasions is to risk opening the door of your life to make the heart connections, to allow your experiences to create a mutual mentoring, such a rare treasure and so difficult to find.

## When and How Does Mentoring Begin?

As folks ask me what this book is about, I tell them, but then return the question: "What does the term *journeymen* say to you, what images come to mind?" Responses invariably include: men on a journey or pilgrimage, like John Bunyan's *Pilgrim's Progress*; and journeymen as referring to the medieval idea of a professional craft passed from master to apprentice. Men often mention sports, where players travel from team to team, or present-day journeymen electricians or masons. (There's a French revival of professional journeymen known as *compagnons*.)

Jesus' word to the lawyer, "Go and do likewise," means that an apprentice is trained through the pain of one's own smarting Samaritan experiences. In *Waiting for God*, the French Jewish Christian mystic Simone Weil observed: "When an apprentice gets hurt, or complains of being tired, the workmen and peasants have this fine expression, 'It is the trade entering his body.'" Aware of our own pain, we are ready to begin "the trade"—the exchange of being mentored and mentoring. It is the axiom of the Twelve-Step programs: Part of our healing is to be a wounded healer for another needy soul.

To practice this trade we need to have mentors. But a man also needs to be a mentor to be whole. In a parking lot after lunch, I recall a friend asking me, "By what age?" I blurted out, "Probably by thirty five." Surprised, he asked, "That young?" I remembered Carl Jung said that by that age every quest is a spiritual one. Jesus died at about thirty-three. And in most cultures around the world even today, by thirty-five a man is considered an elder—and is honored, not shamed, by it. But ask me now by what age, and I will tell you of my son mentoring me. I will answer with Earl R. Henslin in *Man to Man* that to become a mentor is a process beginning early in life and deepening as one matures.

We often hear the refrain, "Where have all the heroes gone?" We have a hard time finding mentors. This is not only because our heroes have feet of clay—they always have. A major difference today is that none of our elders can say to us, "This is the wisdom you need," because no one has been an elder in the twenty-first century before.

"Youth, apprentices, and mentors / Help us learn this craft of faith— / In a guild that spans the centuries, eons, / Leaving footprints on the path." I want to convey two themes here: a sequential movement from learning to eldering, and a cyclical movement, a prayer that the youth, apprentices, and mentors of present, past, and future will learn from each other—a life-giving communion of saints.

Practicing this "trade" goes both directions, helping to shape others and being shaped by them. Committing to a loved one, parenting children, or mentoring others will surely call for occasions when you must pull back from your most treasured values, in order to allow space for those same values to arise in the ones you love. It is the experience of *kenōsis*, the Greek word for Jesus' "self-emptying," (Phil. 2:1-11). In Hebrew tradition it is *tzimtzum*, God "stepping back" from creation to give space to the creatures. It is the essence of mentoring by means of the mentor's own vulnerability. It cuts through the deceit of being an expert example to being a genuine example.

## Jacob Transformed: Model of Male Mentoring

During a crisis, when young Holden Caulfield in J. D. Salinger's *The Catcher in the Rye* is drawn to visit a teacher he has loved, the elderly man affirms him, "Many, many men have been just as troubled morally and spiritually as you are right now. . . . You'll learn from them—if you want to. Just as someday, if you have something to offer, someone will learn something from you. It's a beautiful reciprocal arrangement."[1]

Mentoring is all about reciprocity, using your own struggles to bless, illustrated by three images of Jacob's story: Jacob's ladder with angels ascending and descending at Bethel, Jacob limping away after wrestling all night at the river Jabbok, and Jacob being embraced by his estranged brother, Esau (Gen. 28:10-22; 32:22-21; 33:1-11). In these Jacob provides a model for genuine male spirituality. Here is the wounded healer. The genuine male mentor has struggled with life and God and come away with a limp—with a wound he cannot hide, one that contains its own story, one that embraces self while embracing an "enemy," one that creates new healing every time the story is told.

## The Paschal Mystery: The Crucified-Rising Jesus

Christ "re-deems" men's experiences, to borrow an image from James E. Dittes in *Driven by Hope*. The crucified-rising Jesus is the sign that God deems our surrendered failures, false starts, and limping attempts to climb the ladders of success as valuable steps in this spiritual pilgrimage. Like a failed experiment in a scientific laboratory, every foiled attempt is valued as a notch of spiritual insight on this ladder of learning.

Poet Maya Angelou, speaking in Harrisburg, Pennsylvania, encouraged students not to minimize their life experiences by failing to learn beyond what's taught in the classroom: "Young men and women, you need to know someone was there before you. . . . Someone fell before you and someone miraculously rose before you."

Her words echo the paschal mystery: Christ falling on his way to the cross and rising as the true pattern for all of our mentoring. "Be imitators of me, as I am of Christ," Paul says to the Corinthians (1 Cor. 11:1). To be a mentor is to allow the pattern of Christ's life to take shape in yourself, to surrender your own limping attempts to the mercy of God: "Father, into your hands I commend my spirit" (Luke 23:46). "Go and do likewise" means to allow your surrendered experiences to create life-giving connections for others. It is to surrender to hope.

So the goal of a mentor is not to be perfect. Rather like Jacob or David, Peter or Paul, the genuine example is one who offers one's sins of collusion, control, passivity, and even violence to be exposed to the light and used as a gift for the community. The mark of a genuine mentor is resiliency with love.

### Night Demons

They come in the night,
these demons of self-doubt—
they come to disqualify me,
kidnapping my confidence:
How can you be spiritual
yet be this anxious?
How dare you offer
your needy self to be
a spiritual guide for others?

Then the Spirit comes—
to comfort, to console,
fortifying me with
the ancient assurance
that I am one beggar
showing other beggars
where to find bread,
that my very neediness
validates my credentials,
as one who surely seeks
and just as surely finds—
as one already found.

## Two Notes in Discord: Home and Work

We are always being caught "between two notes, / which are somehow always in discord," in the words of the poet Rainer Maria Rilke. For men, these two conflicting notes often have to do with balancing work and relationships. Thomas J. Watson Jr., father of six children, tells what it used to be like to deal with his feelings at work at IBM and with his family:

> By the time I got home, there would be nothing left of me. I'd walk in and find the usual disorder of a large household— one of the kids had shot a BB gun at a passing car, or two of them were fighting, or somebody had bad grades. These things would strike me as crises that needed to be resolved right away, and yet I had no energy to bring to bear. I'd feel a desperate wish for somebody else to step in and make the decisions so I didn't have to. That's when I'd blow up. The kids would scatter like quail and Olive would catch the brunt of my frustration. . . .[2]

Watson tells how it took him years to see the difference between managing a company and being a father. With the family it was like driving a car with multiple steering wheels:

> I kept trying to exercise more control than I had.
> When I saw I could not bend my wife and children to my will, I'd feel totally thwarted and boxed in. Those were the blackest moments of my adult life. An argument with Olive

and the kids would sometimes make me so morose that the only thing I could do was hole up. I'd lock myself in my dressing room and Olive would stand on the other side of the door and try to get me to come out. Finally, she'd reach the end of her rope. She'd call my brother and say, "Can't you come cheer Tom up?" Dick would come down from New Canaan. He always knew how to make my responsibilities seem lighter and draw me back into the world.[3]

Here was a man living out of the dominative, assertive mode in his work life, and when he tried it in his family relationships and it did not work, he flipped to the impoverished, passive mode. He was blessed that his family did not allow it to work at home, blessed to be holed up in his closet, and blessed to have a mentor in the form of his brother. Strangely, his impoverishment at home began to have an effect on his way of managing IBM.

But the two notes may also be in discord in the mentor-disciple relationship, as Samuel Osherson describes in *Finding Our Fathers*:

The mentoring relationship suffers from the same deficiencies and stresses as other male relationships, particularly those of father and son. Notwithstanding its positive aspects, men often act out in the mentoring relationship unfinished conflicts with their own fathers and families. . . . Some mentors can be unconsciously destructive of their charges, and some mentees can demand an unattainable or inappropriate love from the mentor, which interferes with their work.[4]

Without realizing it, men who live disconnected from their feelings shame their children, loved ones, and colleagues. More than two decades ago Daniel J. Levinson wrote in *The Seasons of a Man's Life* how an intense mentor relationship often ends with conflict and bad feelings on both sides. We should have known this. The disciples were basically disillusioned with their Master.

## The Male Crisis of Mentors

We have run headlong into the male crisis: *We have few models for male mentoring in Western society because the examples of the past are no longer working.* These largely followed a hierarchical style. Learn from a superior and you too will move up the ladder of progress. A mentor was a cultural hero. Bigger equals better. In *Finding Our Fathers,* a young physician describes his frustration:

"I feel like there are mentors to show me how to be a surgeon in the old mold—completely dedicated to my work to the exclusion of everything else, inattentive to other people's feelings and needs, and willing to ruthlessly climb the ladder of success." The young physician stopped for a moment, then plunged on:

"But there aren't mentors, or at least I haven't found them, who can help me become a *feeling, powerful* man, as well as physician."[5]

The problem is finding male mentors who reflect empowering compassion and gentle strength. There have been attempts. Rural and village life used to provide natural ways of passing on traditions from fathers to sons. But with movements of young men from farms to cities, in the mid-nineteenth century the YMCA sprang up to cultivate a "muscular Christianity." The Y, with world leadership from men like John R. Mott, Oswald Chambers, and Amos Alonzo Stagg, and the Boy Scouts, begun by Sir Robert Baden-Powell in Britain, had a similar objective: to help urbane youth to stay physically, mentally, and spiritually fit.

But from the time of World Wars I and II until recently, the military model was largely the dominant masculine metaphor of the rite of what it means to be a white North American male. Of course Native Americans and African Americans have always been marginalized in the United States; even the many who served in the military were rarely recognized by the dominant culture.

In 1971 when my thirty-one-year-old brother died, I recall my sister-in-law being asked by the funeral director if David had ever served in the armed forces. She answered apologetically, "No, because he had fallen arches in his feet." The way the question was asked and the way she responded was a telltale sign of acceptance of the military as the "normal" male American experience; one had to apologize for exceptions.

Historic pacifists—Mennonites, Amish, Brethren, the Friends (Quakers)—were especially marginalized by this prevailing rite of maleness. Yet it was precisely during this militaristic period that these groups pioneered in creating alternative service programs. Today, church- and government-based programs for men and women provide nonmilitary alternatives for serving others while developing tough survival skills and healthy intimacy. Maybe, I ponder, my own family is somehow living out its Anabaptist heritage as younger members take time out from school and work to do service projects in the United States and abroad.

## Models of Mentoring

The Daytime Emmy Awards honored Presbyterian minister Fred Rogers of PBS's *Mister Rogers' Neighborhood* with a Lifetime Achievement Award. His acceptance speech followed a dreary sequence of insults and off-color jokes. In contrast, Rogers asked his audience to take ten seconds to think of "people who helped you become who you are today." As this roomful of TV stars and producers sat in silence, some of them had tears streaming down their faces. Imagine it—just *ten seconds* could bring to the surface such hidden hunger.

People are starving for mentors who connect their inner lives with their outer worlds. Incidentally, Rogers gets up early to engage in prayer and meditation, then before doing laps in the local pool, quietly sings a simple chant, "Jubilate Deo." Anyone reading these pages can do what Fred Rogers did. You can be the catalysts for that hidden wholeness, as Thomas Merton named it, to come to the surface in lecture halls and factories and lunch rooms and board rooms where pastors cannot enter.

As a boy, William Wordsworth experienced such a mentor. Near the beginning of his poem, "The Excursion," he describes an old man who sat day after day under a tree and befriended the youthful but dejected Wordsworth:

> He loved me; from a swarm of rosy boys
> Singled me out, as he in sport would say,
> For my grave looks, too thoughtful for my years.
> As I grew up, it was my best delight
> To be his chosen comrade. Many a time
> On holidays, we rambled through the woods.

## Divine Pattern for Human Mentors

In the Exodus tradition, *God is a journeyer*: "I know their sufferings, and I have come down to deliver them" (Exod. 3:7-8). "So *God led the people by the roundabout way* of the wilderness toward the Red Sea. . . . The LORD *went in front of them* in a pillar of cloud by day, *to lead them along the way,* and in a pillar of fire by night" (Exod. 13:18, 21; italics mine).

The Hebrew Torah (the first five books of the Bible) and the gospel proclaim the same thing: *Jesus embodies a kind of walking-around version of the Torah.* "And the Word became flesh and tented among us" (John 1:14, AT).

God is by nature a journeyer: "I have not lived in a house since the day I brought up the people of Israel from Egypt to this day, but *I have been moving about* in a tent and a tabernacle" (2 Sam. 7:6; italics mine). The danger of temples and churches is that "God" becomes more systematized, nailed down, domesticated, "thingified."

"God on the move" and "God in the temple" will always exist in a genuine paradox, like light which physicists tell us is an unexplainable union of wave *and* particle. At the dedication of this temple King Solomon acknowledges this double reality in his prayer: "Will God indeed reside with mortals on earth? Even heaven and the highest heaven cannot contain you, how much less this house which I have built!" (2 Chron. 6:18). God dwells in the temple but is still on the move far beyond it.

The God of the roundabout journey delights in an unfolding process, in wilderness wanderings as well as the destination. And it is all such a corrective to the distorted male spirituality that would have the angels on Jacob's ladder only *ascending* in a straight line toward heaven with none of them *descending* to the depths. It is a distorted male spirituality that would like to draw a straight line from the land of Egypt to the land of Canaan and bypass the wilderness wanderings. It is the distorted spirituality that would prefer the expressway to the road. For the God of the roundabout journey knows that given an expressway we might easily change our minds and zoom back to slavery (Exod. 13:17).

> God of the mountain, God on the move:
> Strengthen my resolve, hold me in your love.

## Knowing It All vs. Asking Questions

I just conducted informal research with two electricians who came to install a phone jack for my computer modem. Asking for associations with *journeyman*, they readily responded: someone who has completed the training for a trade and is now a professional, ready to teach other apprentices. One spoke of Union standards and of having supervised a Job Corps training program. Then he added, "The biggest sign of a good journeyman is that he's not afraid to ask questions. When they're apprentices they're afraid to ask, so they act like they know it all." The other added, "When we're on a complicated project, we're always gettin' each other's ideas on how to go about it, and it saves time, and then when we're done it wasn't just one guy's thing."

I could not buy such wisdom or find it so well said in my fifty-some books on men's issues. Asking these guys for their ideas conveyed spiritual self-esteem while also gifting myself—so that now I feel a genuine intimacy with them and with God as I am writing this. It was just such wisdom that the poet Rainer Maria Rilke passed on to a younger apprentice in his timeless *Letters to a Young Poet*:

> I want to beg you . . . to be patient toward all that is unsolved in your heart and to try to love the *questions themselves* like locked rooms and like books that are written in a very foreign tongue. Do not now seek the answers, which cannot be given you because you would not be able to live them. And the point is, to live everything. *Live* the questions now. Perhaps you will then gradually, without noticing it, live along some distant day into the answer.[6]

## PRAYER EXERCISE 11: A Child Mentor

Read and meditate on Matthew 18:1-5. Everyone has had experiences of the wisdom of a child bringing one back to the true self. I invite you to recall such an experience now. Then spend a few minutes reflecting on it in your journal. Sometime during this week, find a person or group to whom you can tell it and relive the moment. Use Resource I or if you are in a group use Resource II.

## PRAYER EXERCISE 12: Your Personal Board of Directors

Using your journal, prayerfully reflect over your life. Then create your "personal board of directors." This is not a board that you will actually call together—though some you might. It is an inward constellation of persons who have in common you and your best interest.

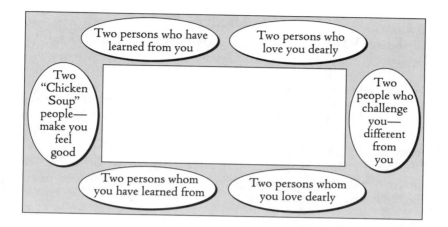

1. Inventory yourself . . . and your board.

2. Think of some recent celebration . . . or crisis. How many did you phone, e-mail, or contact about the celebration or crisis?

3. What are some ways you spend time with your board? How do you pray for them? Keep in touch with them?

OPTION: Create a board of mentors no longer living, who inform your life in various areas: for example, C. S. Lewis, Dorothy Day.

## For Personal Reflection or Group Conversation

1. Reflect on your life mentors. What qualities do you admire in them?

2. Ask yourself: Which qualities would I like to cultivate in my own life? What qualities have others told me they appreciate in me? (If you are in a group, allow each person to reflect in silence. Then turn to one other person and share.)

3. Refer back to Prayer Exercise 12. Find a way to share this in a group or with one of the people on your board. Which positions were most difficult to fill? How many are long term (more than five years)? short-term?

# EXCURSION 5:
# King, Warrior, Magician, Lover—A Christian Lens

As Robert Moore and Douglas Gillette have pointed out in their book by this title, these four qualities of manhood permeate the ancient myths and experiences of men. I admit my first reaction was to blench. Those of us of Anabaptist or Quaker heritage often have difficulty owning raw feelings of power, violence, and sexuality.

Yet the Bible is full of these archetypes. It has helped me to understand the positive and negative aspects of each of the four, to see both the gift and the sin in each.

KING:   Positive—leader, empowerer.
        Negative—tyrant or weakling.

As with Plato's "philosopher king," the wise and good king empowers the people to govern themselves and develop their potential. He is not threatened by issues of control, but rather cultivates love and trust in self and others. By contrast, the unhealthy king operates out of fear, which takes two forms: the tyrant, whose only way to keep peace is by manipulation, domination, and violence; or the weakling, who, unlike the genuinely vulnerable wise king, always needs to look strong because he is weak. Captain Edward J. Smith of the *Titanic* provides a classic example of the weakling: so insecure that he accepted the dare to be famous by arriving at New York City early, thus firing up the extra engines to give the illusion of power—yet totally passive as hundreds plunged to their deaths. The weak king does as much violence by default as the tyrant does by deliberate intent. Jesus is the ideal Royal Prototype—the Servant-Lord, whose "kingdom" is the "commonwealth of heaven," where the last shall be first.

WARRIOR:   Positive— pioneer, preservationist.
           Negative—sadist or masochist.

The healthy warrior takes joy in defending the best qualities of the king out of love and trust. The unhealthy warrior is defensive, fighting out of fear, which takes two forms: the sadist, whose only method of defense is to wound and violate others; or the masochist, who engages in self-demeaning behavior, thus defending the unhealthy king by needing and getting sympathy. "The pen is mightier than the sword" can be a healthy warrior's way of fighting. The crucified Jesus takes on the pain, violence, and conflict of others in such a way that it is transformed into positive energy in the resurrection.

MAGICIAN: Positive—visionary, genius.
        Negative—manipulator or withholder.

The good magician, like the Magi in Scripture, is the visionary for the king. The good teacher is always happy when the student excels, when the child becomes greater than the parent. The unhealthy magician manipulates the student for the teacher's glory, or withholds information, fearing the student will surpass the teacher. Jesus is the Master Teacher: "I do not call you servants any longer, because the servant does not know what the master is doing; but I have called you friends, because I have made known to you everything that I have heard from my Father" (John 15:15). Christ Jesus "became for us wisdom [*sophia*] from God" (1 Cor. 1:30), and "Wisdom [*sophia*] is justified by all her children" (Luke 7:35, RSV). Caring children and sound students are the wise elder's legacy.

LOVER: Positive—artist, romantic.
        Negative—addicted lover; impotent or innocent one.

The healthy lover expresses love and intimacy in ways that liberate both parties. The unhealthy lover needs the other because he cannot love without keeping another in chains, and thus is addicted to his passions, or he thinks that stifling his passion is the way to be righteous. The priest and the Levite in the story of the Good Samaritan represent the "innocent ones," impotent but intent on "doing it right." Jesus, who consistently allowed himself to be interrupted to show compassion, and whose own death is referred to as his "passion," points to the Samaritan: "He had compassion" (Luke 10:33, KJV).

    Which of these four is more developed in your life? Which needs attention? healing?

8

# Male Sexuality
## Men and Intimacy

In general, most men do not have an intimate male friend of
the kind that they recall fondly from boyhood or youth.
—Daniel Levinson, *The Seasons of a Man's Life*

You have never felt completely safe in your body.
—Henri J. M. Nouwen, *The Inner Voice of Love*

The union of the mathematician with the poet, fervor with
measure, passion with correctness, this surely is the ideal.
—William James, "Collected Essays and Reviews"

In his February 1997 letter to members, Sierra Club President Adam
Werbach related "a cautionary tale for our times." Researchers, he
reported, went to a preschool and asked the youngsters, "Who knows
how to sing?" Everyone's hand shot up. "Who knows how to dance?"
They waved their hands enthusiastically. "Who knows how to draw?"
Again all hands went up. The next week, the researchers posed the
same questions to a class of college students. "Who knows how to
sing?" A few hands were raised. "Who knows how to dance?" Two
hands shyly went up. "Draw?" No response.

Somewhere between preschool and so-called higher education we
lose track of vital means of self-expression. No wonder we resort so
readily to anger. And surely the few college students to raise their
hands were mostly women. What of a time when a majority of men
were drummers, balladeers, storytellers, dancers, and pray-ers?

## Journeymen: The Craft of Leading the Nonsplit Life

I think of an amazing exception to Werbach's cautionary tale. For decades the maverick baseball announcer, Harry Caray, dared to belt his off-key voice through a microphone, inviting the masses to sing along with him at the seventh-inning stretch: "Take me out to the ball game!" When he died in 1998, commentators pointed out how Caray's willingness to offer his own gravelly voice validated singing for all who thought they could not sing. Here was a prophetic example of being a fool for the sake of others—dare I say a fool for Christ's sake. For wherever we see a comic coming together of opposites that offers healing, there is the hidden Messiah at work in the world, without glory. Caray's simple legacy embodies a unity between healthy sports, a major means of male self-expression, and music, which culture defines as more feminine. And if we cannot find William James's ideal unity between mathematician and poet, at least we could make friends in both camps. *Journeymen are those who practice the craft of leading the nonsplit life.*

Especially for men, culture promotes the rift between sacred and secular, sports and arts, task and relationships, sexuality and spirituality. Yet the Incarnation means "the Word became flesh" (John 1:14). Jesus Christ is the embodiment of the unity of the very things that threaten to tear us apart. The worldly becomes holy. To discern how to live in Christ is countercultural: "I appeal to you, therefore, brothers and sisters, by the mercies of God, to present your bodies as a living sacrifice, holy and acceptable to God, which is your spiritual worship. Do not be conformed to this world, but be transformed by the renewing of your minds, so that you may discern what is the will of God" (Rom. 12:1-2).

We are not disembodied spirits. That is an underlying heresy of gnosticism and many of its New Age variations, to spiritualize the physical. But what does it mean to live and pray incarnationally? In order to present your body to God, you need to begin by being present to your body.

I was the only male participant in a group of two dozen women, and we were discussing a statement from a personal journal of Henri J. M. Nouwen, recorded in *The Inner Voice of Love*: "You have never felt completely safe in your body." Women were commenting on their fear of being violated, intruded upon. Suddenly it occurred to me that my fear of not being safe in my body as a male is that it can so easily do the invading, that my body might burst forth and do things I do not want it to—impulsively, physically, verbally, nonverbally. It was an Aha! moment for all in the room, including myself: two differing ways of experiencing fear of the body.

Put in a crude way, because our culture stifles natural artistic expression especially among males, why are we surprised that so many men find sexual acting out or fighting their only ways to deal with the body's caged energies? But if we never feel completely safe in our bodies, what are we so afraid of? In the hit movie *Moonstruck*, the frustrated character played by Olympia Dukakis keeps asking, "Why do men chase women?" The answer: "Because they're afraid of death." In French, we can see a connection with the very term for intercourse: *le petit mors*, the little death.

An old adage says, "A woman gives sex hoping for love; a man gives love hoping for sex." One fears not being loved; the other fears being mortal—whether it is a woman or a man. Is there not a way to love your neighbor *as* yourself?

## Mystical Sexuality

If journeymen are to practice the craft of a nonsplit life, then the intensity of male sexual passion cannot be separated from our deepest spiritual hungers, woundings, and bliss. The intricate connection of sexuality and spirituality is both frightening and exhilarating. It is a terrific thing—terrific as in wonderful, yet also terrifying.

And in sexual passion we really experience "the little death"—a temporary detachment from "things" in a moment of bliss. But *blesser* in French means "to bless" but also "to wound": Jacob is blessed *and* wounded. And our sexuality is often a primary way of our wounding others or being wounded.

In Hebrew and Greek the same verb for *knowing* is used to refer to spiritual *and* sexual intimacy. "Now the man *knew* his wife Eve, and she conceived and bore Cain" (Gen. 4:1); "Be still, and *know* . . ." (Ps. 46:10). "I want *to know* Christ and the power of his resurrection and the sharing of his sufferings by becoming like him" (Phil. 3:10, all italics mine).

The place for training ministers is a theological *seminary*—where the "seeds" of faith will germinate and bear fruit. And while seminary is a male symbol, a primary symbol in every local church is feminine. The baptismal font represents the womb as the church becomes the place where Christ is born again and again in its members.

Sexual imagery has been used by countless mystics to express the sweetness of communion with the Lord—as in this classic verse attributed to Bernard of Clairvaux:

> Jesus, the very thought of Thee
> With sweetness fills my breast,
> But sweeter far Thy face to see
> And in Thy presence rest.

The Song of Solomon may have been written simply as a love song, yet both Jewish and Christian mystics (like Bernard and John of the Cross) have seen in it a romantic ecstasy with God. And ec-stasy is what we experience in sexual passion—a sense of "going outside the self." In John of the Cross we see this mystical sexuality beautifully expressed:

> One dark night,
> Fired with love's urgent longings
> —Ah, the sheer grace!—
> I went out unseen,
> My house being now all stilled. . . .
>
> I abandoned and forgot myself
> Laying my face on my beloved;
> All things ceased; I went out from myself,
> Leaving my cares
> Forgotten among the lilies.[1]

Sexual self-expression in solitude can be offered as prayer in communion and intercession for all creation—simultaneously loving God, neighbor, and self. Sometimes such expressions take the form of poetry or hymns, music or art. John's poem expresses an experience of genuine altruism the self-conscious ego dies: "He wounded my neck / With his gentle hand / Suspending all my senses."[2] We can also experience mystical sexuality in very concrete forms of service: compassion for an abused child or passion for a social cause. In acts of self-forgetting love, endorphins are released akin to the experience of orgasm.

Through spiritual intimacy with Christ, many men and women have found positive sublimation for an empty marriage, a boring job, or co-dependent relationships, intimacy that allowed them to go on living and loving with hope.

## Nongenital Ways to Express Our Sexuality

If we would cultivate alternative ways of expressing our sexuality, it would help us deal with our primal fear of death and our pent-up energies in ways other than violating the earth and its inhabitants. Before reading on, I invite you to Prayer Exercise 13: What are some creative, nongenital expressions of your sexuality?

When I ask this in my classes and retreats, answers come back faster than I can record them on newsprint:

| | | |
|---|---|---|
| Color, light, | Intimacy—with | creativity. |
| poetry, art. | God, self, others: | Mystical |
| Nature: | prayer, | experiences, |
| a sunset, | meditation. | sense of wonder. |
| a rosebud, | Reading, writing, | Photography, |
| the night sky, | storytelling. | music, |
| the ocean, | Sports, tai chi, | letter writing, |
| mountain | yoga, karate. | bread baking. |
| climbing, | Altruism, | Dreams, |
| swimming, | empathy, | tears, |
| fishing. | listening, | touch, |
| Humor, comedy. | contemplation, | sound. |

These represent only a tiny microchip of the healthy ways we can experience our spiritual-sexual oneness with God and the universe. How does your list compare with the one above? As Elizabeth Barrett Browning said it, "How do I love thee? Let me count the ways." If men (and women) would nurture such manifold ways of expressing love of God, neighbor, and self, we would place less of a burden on our partners to fulfill all our sexual needs and be less likely to engage in outside sexual affairs to prove our genital prowess.

Impoverishment of the male soul can be extreme. Such poverty of inner resources can occur that his only form of physical expression becomes either rape or self-punishment. As I share a few of my own non-genital experiences below, I invite you to make your own connections.

*Intercourse* in Older English was a term meaning "intimate conversation," from which a small town near Lancaster, Pennsylvania, gets its unique name. I grew up not far from Intercourse, hearing all the jokes about the name, yet even as a child I somehow understood its double meaning. And though in some ways I felt culturally deprived by not watching TV or movies or traveling on family vacations, yet I experienced the rich treasures of a natural sex education. One day a visiting friend from Baltimore yelled from the barn, "Kent, come look! The bull has a big carrot!" Seeing the bull masturbate or mount a cow was nothing new for me, nor was watching the procedure of artificial insemination that eventually replaced the bull. And I recall explaining sex quite scientifically to my city friend—a bigger thrill for me than telling a dirty joke.

As a young father, I will always treasure the intimacy of evenings when I put our children to bed, engaging in Share and Prayer with a Child, or when I took them out to eat, one-on-one. (See Prayer Exercise 19.) One evening I was putting our younger daughter to bed during daylight saving time, when she looked up at me with saucer-eyes and said: "How come after I play so hard all day I'm so wide awake every night, and after I sleep so hard all night I'm so tired every morning?" What if I had not been there to hear, like the tree falling in the forest, the sound of that childlike wisdom? You cannot buy such moments. In *The Wild Man's Journey*, Franciscan Richard Rohr reports an informal study conducted by a priest. Sadly the study showed that less than one percent of children experienced their fathers praying with them. It is not too late; you can try Share and Prayer with a grandchild, or with kids in a Sunday school class. Or conduct a survey in your own church and share the results to raise the awareness of other fathers.

In one single moment we may experience simultaneously several of these ways of loving and being loved. I was driving with a Swiss friend to Chautauqua Institution, New York (a weekend President Clinton was there, as it turned out), then on to Niagara Falls, Canada. But the real high point happened while driving into the night when my friend noticed the most spectacular sky, which I could not appreciate while driving. He exclaimed in German, "*Die Milchstraße!* What do you say in English, the Milky Street?" We pulled off for a major reststop, got out of the car, and stood transfixed beneath the deep Elk County, Pennsylvania, sky—watching the Milky Way with no competing city lights, no noise. In that rarefied moment, embraced by light years of time, we were one with each other and the universe. It was like a cosmic orgasm. Though our bodies did not touch, scientifically they were silently releasing health-producing endorphins. This is happening for me again even as I recollect that moment. On our return trip, even with a clear sky, nature provided no such spectacular show.

These moments are pure miracle when they happen and you "kiss the joy as it flies," as the poet William Blake wrote.

These experiences of male intimacy cut across all our pigeonholes of gender, sexual-orientation, race, age, or education. I invite you to recall specific experiences such as the ones I have just recounted.

## Male-Female Experience Revisited

During a retreat, I invited folks to trace the outline of their left or right hand in a journal, then in silence to notice associations for various fingers, palm, joints. Afterward, as we reflected one-on-one, I showed the woman next to me how I had drawn lines on the palm of mine and written the word *linear*; instantly she held out her palm and said, "That's interesting, I think of *round, saucer!*" It is a tiny experiment, but it illustrates in a simple way that an initial response even from a sensitized male like myself was linear, while that of a female was circular.

So "masculine" ways of knowing are generally more exterior, linear, and sequential like steps on a ladder, as reflected in John of the Cross: "I went out unseen, / My house being now all stilled. / In darkness, and secure, / By the secret ladder. . . ."[3] And as a contemporary book title illustrates, *Women's Ways of Knowing*[4] are more interior, repetitive, and cyclical, as reflected in Teresa of Avila's *Interior Castle*. (See chapter 2.)

It is not surprising that "masculine-type" spiritual experiences tend to be more dramatic, with qualities of being subdued: Jacoblike wrestlings in the night, Jonahlike drownings, Paul-like Damascus road turnarounds. "Feminine-type" spiritual experiences tend to be more gradual, with qualities of being receptive: Hannahlike and Marylike, "Here am I, the servant of the Lord." But these are only "types": Paul could accept and validate the youthful Timothy's growing faith experience from the knees of his grandmother Lois and his mother Eunice (2 Tim. 1:5; 3:14-15). Both "Paul" and "Timothy" Christians need each other. And some Timothy types like myself never knew the time when we were not a Christian, yet in later life experienced a traumatic reconversion—an "angel on the descent."

Though these perspectives are complementary, there are significant differences. As I mentioned earlier, studies of the brain have reported that men tend to process information quickly but separately (language and logic in the left sphere; arts and music in the right); women tend to process it cyclically and more gradually, back and forth. This says at least four things:

1.  Men's gift under pressure is a quick response, *to rise to the occasion*, exemplified by the male phallic responsiveness. "Courage is grace under pressure," as Dorothy Parker aptly said it, and men's courageous haste needs grace if it is not to be invasive.

2.  As males we need to *cultivate intentional silences*, pauses that allow for this integrative processing to take place in the brain, to sanctify "downtime"; the penis is soft and still more than it is hard and intense.

3.  The spheres of the brain, like our male anatomy, teach us that *authentic males are spherical as well as linear*. We have scrotal, testicular energy: capacity for containing and protecting silent, hidden seed, ripening through long-term patience.

4.  Our rapid responses need the *balancing of the community* under pressure—much like the image of an emergency room represented in the TV show *ER*, where multiple decisions are being made simultaneously and immediately, allowing for a rapid team response that multiplies the effectiveness of any single individual.

## Sexuality as Vocational Generativity

In the Bible, "Be fruitful and multiply" does not just mean having babies. One's life is meant to bear the fruits of love, and fecundity requires painful pruning "to make it bear more fruit" (John 15:1-5). The grain of wheat must fall into the ground and "die"—then "it bears much fruit" (John 12:24). The tree of life produces twelve kinds of fruit, "and the leaves of the tree are for the healing of the nations" (Rev. 22:2). This final chapter of the Bible tells us that the most powerful way our sexuality can be expressed is when the little deaths of this life are transformed into a positive contribution to justice and peace.

The life of Mohandas Gandhi provides such an example. John R. Mott, an early leader of the YMCA movement, once asked Gandhi what was the most meaningful experience of his life. Gandhi proceeded to tell about his trip from Durban, Natal, to Maritzburg, Natal, South Africa, where on arrival a white man entered the train, and

Gandhi, holding a first-class ticket, was told he must leave. He quietly stated that he had ridden first class from Durban, showed the conductor his ticket, and said they would have to forcibly remove him. This they proceeded to do. It was winter and freezing cold in this mountainous station, and Gandhi was now separated from his luggage and warm clothing. That mortifying night Gandhi became intimate with oppressed peoples of the whole world. That night would give birth to the concept of *satyagraha*—soul force, or nonviolence.[5] And Gandhi's life is still bearing fruit.

Here is the paschal mystery of death-dealing experiences begetting life, the Messiah still at work secretly, without glory. The most profound expression of this sexual-spiritual-political mystery is when "your deep gladness and the world's deep hunger meet," as Frederick Buechner wrote in *Wishful Thinking*.

In Hebrew tradition there's a fine phrase that expresses our vocation in the world: *tikkun olam*, meaning "to repair the universe." Once when I was leading a workshop on discernment and vocation, a woman from Canada told us how a therapist had helped her find such a satisfying paraphrase of *tikkun olam* to express her own vocation: "to mend the torn fabric of the universe."

I could not wait to share the interpretation with a rabbi friend back home. Over lunch, we pondered, it seemed like an ideal feminine translation; could there be a more masculine counterpart? One Saturday morning while listening to the National Public Radio show *Car Talk*, where two brothers beat up on each other and spill forth more male humor working on relationships than they do fixing cars, it occurred to me. A guy's version of *tikkun olam* could be "to rebuild the broken transmission of the universe"!

We might also ponder that many of the world's tailors and weavers are men, and that we need to weave a blend of soft and hard images to transmit empowering love: to mend the torn fabric, as well as to repair the broken transmission. And we guys, whose natural propensity is to want to fix things, could learn a lesson from the whole ambiance of the show. On *Car Talk* cars are merely the "vehicle" for talk, for lonely people to work on their relationships using male humor to do it.

Genital images in dreams are often symbols of a spiritual vocation, which illustrates the bankruptcy of a purely literal or Freudian approach to such dreams. Many of my dreams have symbols of my writing in them. Here is one: *I dream that a wealthy older woman gives me a gold fountain pen. I am a bit self-conscious about using it.*

Wanting meaning from this dream, in my journal I actually drew the fountain pen, colors and all. Immediately I was stuck by the phallic similarity and symmetry. The dream calls me to use this gold given to me by the old woman (my inner wisdom), but I can be a bit too modest about using this gift. Writing is a "seminal" way for me to be generative. The dream is still vivid. In times of unbearable discouragement, the image serves as God's inner prodding me to continue writing—which is surely one way my complex sexual-spiritual soul becomes intimate with the world. The inner ecstasy I experience is palpable when someone tells me that disclosing the vulnerable space in my heart through my writing has created a healing experience.

Whenever we are lovingly present to someone beyond time and space in some way, we participate in the resurrection existence of Christ, who could appear behind locked doors and offer peace. Whenever we become aware of such times, we experience heaven now.

## PRAYER EXERCISE 13: Praying Our Sexuality

Begin with silent prayer. Contemplate: What are some nongenital expressions of my sexuality? Spend about five minutes in silence. In your journal begin listing them. Looking over your own list and the list on page 103, celebrate these ways that you experience intimacy with God and creation. Prayerfully contemplate some areas you would like to develop to enrich your life, noting these in your journal.

## For Personal Reflection or Group Conversation

1. What would it mean "to lead a nonsplit life"? How would this congruent life affect your relationships at home? at work? in your personal life? What might you do differently, give up, or take on?

2. "In the Bible, 'Be fruitful and multiply' does not just mean having babies." What are nonbiological ways that you can see generativity in your life? Consider not only people whose lives you have touched, but ideas and projects to which you have "given birth."

# RESTSTOP 3:
## Washing the Ring Out of the Tub

B ack in the 1970s, while driving home to small-town Waynesboro, Pennsylvania, from Baltimore, I recall listening to a cassette lecture about marriage by an older Catholic priest. If it had not been a long trip, I would probably have judgmentally turned it off as I thought, *What's this guy know about marriage anyway?* At some point he began to talk about washing the ring out of the bathtub. Again, I dismissed him: *Ah, he's from another generation; we use a shower.* Fortunately I continued to listen. What he was proposing was that washing the ring out of the bathtub, especially for the male partner, might be a way to prepare for lovemaking!

Fortunately, I did not discount the priest that summer afternoon. I have recounted this story countless times in marital counseling, in sermons, in retreats, in conversations. I have coined a phrase for washing out the ring—"holistic foreplay"! It has become for me a metaphor of love and relationships, and often informs my actions.

Somewhere along the way, I realized I was complaining fairly often about the dirty bathrooms in our house. Then it occurred to me that early in our marriage, when I was a seminary student and my wife taught school, I did a good deal of the housekeeping. I remembered the priest's lecture that I had told to so many others—about cleaning the bathtub. "I'll clean the bathrooms!" I proclaimed to myself one night. I began to dedicate the weekly project as a prayer for my two nieces and nephew, a time to remember them and how hard they work. And since the other four members in my own family rarely seemed to notice, I appreciated how women often feel about housework. I began to fold the toilet paper in a little triangle the way they do in fancy hotels, so someone would notice! In these ways I made a game of it.

Today is a Saturday when I had hoped to begin writing early. But at breakfast, my wife informed me that the toilet flusher handle had broken. I already knew that the kitchen-sink sprayer had also broken, along with the fan in the bathroom. *No better time for these projects*, I reasoned. So I took off to the plumbing supply store, admittedly with some irritation. But there were no long lines, and the store had exactly the items I needed.

At the checkout counter, a man mentioned being married for thirty-five years, the clerk said she had been married for thirty-two, and by deduction with my poor math we reasoned I had been married for thirty-three—quite a combined total for three couples these days. Each mentioned some learning: "A lot of stuff you thought was important just isn't," and, "You keep focusing on what's good." Instantly I thought about how I had just cleaned the bathrooms at home and was here doing this "waste work" instead of writing. I said, "And I've discovered that cleaning the bathrooms can be foreplay for good sex!" They lighted up, and I told how I was writing on male spirituality, thanking them for providing me with more research for this book.

This incident reminded me of that story by the priest, and any irritation I had vanished. Like men and women in Studs Terkel's book *Working*, I knew that standing there I was doing two things at once: I was writing this book and I was fixing the plumbing at the same time. It had not been an interruption.

This is a paradigm of male spirituality, where so often our work is such a big part of our lives and we resent it. It is my prayer for each man (and any woman) who reads this: that what you love in life can be wed with the most menial "waste work" you have to do. It is the essence of what Jean-Pierre de Caussade wrote in his little classic *The Sacrament of the Present Moment*. It is Benedictine spirituality—to see no split between the sacrament at the altar and plumbing or conversing in hardware store or writing a book or making love. And men sharing housework may be one of our most revolutionary acts.

I recommend finding a playful way "to wash the ring out of the bathtub"—however you translate it in your relationships. Some such menial service is a way of praying for your lover or someone you would like to love you more. It is a marvelous example of the Reality of joy and sacrifice in the experience of Communion.

# Esau Embraces Jacob

## A New Male Collage

*Roads less traveled, roads not taken,*
*Family pain and foiled careers,*
*Yet in Christ an ending is a beginning*
*Of a whole new layer of years.*
　　*—Guide Us All On This Day Journey*

It was worth a wound—it was worth many wounds—to know the depth of loyalty and love which lay behind that cold mask. The clear, hard eyes were dimmed for a moment, and the firm lips were shaking. For the one and only time I caught a glimpse of a great heart as well as of a great brain.
　　*—Watson, after being wounded, describing Sherlock Holmes in "The Adventure of the Three Garridebs"*

While driving back with my older daughter to Pennsylvania from Asheville, North Carolina, where she was settling into a new home and I had spent some days writing, we listened to Willa Cather's book *O Pioneers!* on cassette. This tragic, romantic story of life in transition between the old world of Europe and the newly emerging world in Nebraska has long held a fascination for me.

One thing came through clearly. Apart from the common factor of being pioneers in a new land that seems as hostile as it does adventurous, the men in this story are as diverse in their attitudes toward life as the countries and the careers from which they have come. Through the eyes of the Bergson family we meet the Swedes, with their natural tendencies for introversion, withdrawal, and persistence. And like the older sibling in the parable of the Prodigal Son, they mostly resent the free-spirited attitude of their Bohemian neighbors, who in turn consider these quiet folks dull and boring.

Even in this one Swedish family we can see these two contrasting archetypes. After John Bergson's death in his forties, his oldest child, the heroine teenager, Alexandra, is left in charge of the farm and her three younger brothers. The older brothers, Oscar and Lou, work Esaulike outside in the fields, but grow to resent Alexandra, though benefiting from her successful leadership. And the very youngest, Emil, is the one destined to receive the choice, Jacoblike "insider" blessing of a college education with an eye to an easier life. It is young Emil Bergson who, Prodigal-like, falls in love with the Bohemian culture and one of its beautiful though unfortunately married women. Tragically, in the end Emil is murdered, and the two brothers refuse to speak to Alexandra. In their eyes she had condoned Emil's prodigal life, and on top of that she was herself considering marriage to an artist whom they saw as a threat to their security.

It is as if all three brothers have lost their souls. The enviable success of their elder sister only highlights the classic absence of a father and male mentor. Older brothers Oscar and Lou cannot find the traditional source of male identity through their own hard work because it gets swallowed up in their hostile attitude toward their elder sister's leadership. And young Emil, who wants to celebrate the gifts of world travel and learning, finds his brothers and his Swedish community unable to validate his searching soul. Here in this one family we see the classic biblical sibling dynamics reenacted, like the ancient Jacoblike and Esaulike warring factions.

## The Fragmented Male Soul

Is this not precisely our current predicament? Many men who once drew their identity from hard work and industry or from Bohemian arts and creativity now feel powerless in the face of changing gender roles and technological obsolescence. While *O Pioneers!* is set at the turn of the nineteenth century, "prodigal" Emil and his "perfectionist" older brothers Oscar and Lou represent an updated version of Luke's parable for our own twenty-first century (Luke 15:11-32). In our time, the unhealthy and unreconciled sides of the dominative-assertive male and passive-impoverished male kill each other off, and tear the male soul apart internally.

This is the core message of the popular British film, *The Full Monty*, where men who in the fifties had prospered in the steel town of Sheffield, England, now find themselves supplanted and unemployed in the late nineties. With women now bringing home more money than steelworkers, these impoverished males try to assert a modicum of creativity by resorting to what is admittedly a shaming experience of offering themselves as male strippers. The film is a pathetic and prophetic statement about the crisis of the impoverished male soul, desperately trying to "erect" a bridge somewhere between shame and violence. As in every crisis, the true prophet seeks to point out the opportunity within the danger of the predicament.

In the twenty-first century, must Cain still resort to striking out at Abel and killing family relationships, as in *O Pioneers!*? Must we find no road to our own identity but by shaming ourselves and our loved ones, as in *The Full Monty*? Like Noah's sons, must we shame a drunken father or innocently turn our backs on our brothers—or our own impoverished souls? And must this death-dealing shame be passed on generation after generation (Gen. 9:20-27)?

Youth who kill flip from passive shame to violent aggression—whether in Jonesboro, Arkansas, or in Littleton, Colorado. After looking at the notebook writings of a fourteen-year-old killer, his school principal said he found a boy who felt weak and powerless, with an angry desire to lash out at the world. Here is a genuine wake-up call for us to find new patterns for being men, being Christian. What does it say that these episodes often occur when our nation is engaging in bombing abroad—while telling youth to solve their problems constructively? What does it say that all these young murderers to date have been males? Some are from violent homes. But several have been active in our churches, sons of deacons or ministers, kids known to be "kind." How does a teenage boy reared in a peace-loving Mennonite home near Lancaster, Pennsylvania, murder his parents?

Here is a clarion call for male spiritual mentors to model for the next generation how to nurture a creative balance of healthy, appropriate assertiveness and healthy appropriate passiveness.

How do we do this? The French concept of *pastiche* refers to the repetitive imitation of great artists by the pupil—writer, musician, painter, mason, athlete, sculptor—until the pupil hones a genuine style of his or her own. You are apprentices of the Master: Keep practicing *pastiche* until the Christ is uniquely and genuinely reproduced in you.

## Jacob and Esau Embrace: A Model of Male Wholeness

"Esau ran to meet [Jacob], and embraced him, and fell on his neck and kissed him, and they wept." Then we see Jacob's response: "Truly to see your face is like seeing the face of God—since you have received me with such favor" (Gen. 33:4, 10). In this forgiving embrace we see the union of empowering compassion and courageous humility—a dramatic embodiment of the key theme of estrangement and reconciliation that runs throughout scripture, uniting the feeling of power with the power of feeling.

We see this empowering compassion and courageous humility in the reunion of Joseph and his estranged brothers:

> Then Joseph said to his brothers, "Come closer to me." And they came closer. He said, "I am your brother, Joseph, whom you sold into Egypt. And now do not be distressed, or angry with yourselves, because you sold me here; for God sent me before you to preserve life." . . . And he kissed all his brothers and wept upon them; and after that his brothers talked with him (Gen. 45:4-5; 15).

One line in this text that we ought to ponder: "And they came closer." What areas of your life come to mind when you think of "coming closer"? (See Prayer Exercise 15.)

We see this empowering compassion and courageous humility in the reunion of the Prodigal with his father: "But while he was still far off, his father saw him and was filled with compassion; he ran and put his arms around him and kissed him" (Luke 15:20). And will the Prodigal be reconciled to his angry brother? We are left to finish the collage with the bits and pieces of our own family albums.

What would it mean if the free-spirited Bohemian and the dutiful Swede within each of us could embrace? What would it mean for the Prodigal and the Perfectionist to mine the treasures from each other's experiences—gifts out of the wild man's journey and the angry man's stuckness?

What would it mean if we began to live out of this new art form, to integrate the feeling of power with the power of feeling? In the eighties I read to my children from Lee Iococca's autobiography where he spoke of his Italian expression of emotion with his father. I announced that I, too, would be kissing and hugging them in public no matter how grown-up they became.

We see this empowering compassion and courageous humility the crucial gesture where Jesus stretched out his arms on the cross to embrace even his enemies: "Abba, forgive them; for they do not know what they are doing" (Luke 23:34, AT). What would it mean to wrestle through our dark nights of self-doubt and hostility, then in the daytime to embrace the enemy within and the enemy without?

We see this empowering compassion and courageous humility again in the crucial gesture where Jesus stretched out his arms on the cross to embrace the absence: "My God, my God, why have you forsaken me?" (Mark 15:34). And where Jesus surrendered to hope: "Abba, into your hands I commend my spirit" (Luke 23:46, AT).

For men to live out of this new art form would mean embracing the warring or impoverished parts of their own souls, and simultaneously fostering relationships with men and women wildly different from themselves. It would mean cultivating an awareness and appreciation of the creative continuum of the seemingly warring opposites and unconscious extremes in our lives:

## Warrior Lover Twins

"Truly to see you is like
seeing the face of God."

Ah when, how can
smooth Jacob and hairy Esau
finally meet to embrace
and bless each other—
privileged impoverished
begging gifting
conservative liberals
sporting arting
spiritual politics
scheming forgiving
high tech high touch?

What would these
warrior lover twins
look like if ever they could
hold one another—
tough tender
wrestling mystics

dreaming disciplined
sweaty thinkers
competitively cooperatively
leading while letting go
with vulnerable strength?

"Truly to see you is like
seeing the face of God."

This is not just a plea for accountants to become Renaissance men or for jocks to value liberal arts. It is a call to embody the Incarnation of Jesus as Messiah, the Word made flesh, the divine-human One who came to reconcile and bless these competing parts of our souls and our society.

## Male Integrity, Christian Spirituality

I have just returned from using a gold-colored marker to put the street numbers on a new mailbox that I received as a Father's Day gift. Pushing hard on the marker, I was sure it was empty, no good. Then in a moment I remembered how I use it when mounting icons on wood blocks. Lightening my touch, I saw the numbers come out beautiful and glossy. Once again, I recognized my "male" tendency to push, and the needed wholeness of lightening up. It is a simple example of how we do violence to others by being heavy-handed—consider them no good when actually they may be filled with gold.

But you may be asking, What makes this a uniquely "Christian" spirituality, not a mere adjustment of the yin-and-yang ingredients in one's life? And what makes this a uniquely "male" spirituality? The answer to the one leads to the other.

As we have seen in earlier chapters, males have a tendency toward outward and linear experiences and toward splitting these seeming opposites from each other. So it is easy to discount another who differs from one's own personality type or social preference. Like Jacob and Esau we can intentionally cultivate relationships with contrasting personalities and groups, and by valuing each other embrace hidden parts of ourselves and thereby become more whole.

A "re-deemed" athletic male may never become an artist, and an artistic male may never become an athlete. But the athlete may begin to practice his sport as an art, and the artist's work may begin to reflect athletic images.

To live in Christ is to begin living out this kind of risk-taking and re-deeming faith, valuing other people and life experiences that the world wants to dismiss—and that is uniquely Christian. It is not a matter of bland balancing but of transformation. In the cross, weakness becomes strength, foolishness becomes wisdom (1 Cor. 1:25).

It is "the mystery hidden for ages"—that Christ "has broken down the dividing wall, that is, the hostility between us" so that "the wisdom of God in its rich variety might now be made known" (Eph. 2:14, 3:9).

We can see this integrity in Jesus who integrated in his own life the rugged male individualism of John the Baptist, with the virtues of wildness and withdrawal, and also the intimacy of John the beloved disciple, with the virtues of gentleness and closeness. I see this congruence in the Promise Keeper movement. Men have come back from its rallies committed to pray for and make friends with someone outside their own cultural or racial circle. And I have witnessed them doing it, while I often hear their critics merely talking about it. Yet any hint of dangerous male superiority—men becoming gentler in order to exercise subtle control over their loved ones, rather than empowering love—must be rejected. When God says to Eve regarding her husband in Genesis 3:16, "And he shall rule over you," such male domination is a direct result of the Fall into sin. "Ruling over" is not the ideal of reciprocal partnership in Genesis 2:18 that mirrors God's own self as expressed in original creation in Genesis 1:27: "So God created humankind in [God's] image, . . . male and female [God] created them." And as C. S. Lewis pointed out in *The Weight of Glory*, equality and democracy are even more necessary after the Fall to protect us from the danger of absolute power-over relationships.

Christ came to re-deem women and men with our original value of uniqueness and equality, and to eradicate any human barriers created by racial, political, or sexual differences: "For all of you are one [equal] in Christ Jesus" (Gal. 3:28). Christ came to restore the "trade" of mutual give-and-take: "Be subject to one another out of reverence for Christ" (Eph. 5:21).

## Transformative Spirituality

This chapter title could be What Will the Integrated Male Look Like? But then, if there is ever one homogenized male mold, we would look like the automated robots in Aldous Huxley's *Brave New World*.

For Christ, the Savior and Pattern, is unique, and so calls each of us to live out our uniqueness within community.

A transformative male spirituality does not mean getting all our differences "fixed" or "made normal," and it does not mean everyone becoming either macho or tender. Instead a maturing male spirituality begins with awareness and ends in trusting the Spirit to use one's distinctive genetic qualities and family systems and Jacoblike limps to create a bearer of God's redemptive grace. It is not so much a stance of self-confidence as God-confidence, a trust in the One who re-deems people and uses experiences that our culture considers wasteful or negative.

After being wounded by gunfire, Watson, Sherlock Holmes' assistant, now lauds the ideal mentor:

> It was worth a wound—it was worth many wounds—to know the depth of loyalty and love which lay behind that cold mask. The clear, hard eyes were dimmed for a moment, and the firm lips were shaking. For the one and only time I caught a glimpse of a great heart as well as of a great brain.[1]

We catch a glimpse of the integrated male: "Christ the Savior and Pattern: Healing wounds, empowering love."

What if our personal vulnerabilities and cultural liabilities can become a source of life-giving faith, hope, and love for others—like the risen Jesus' inviting doubting Thomas to touch his wounds (John 20:24-29)?

What if God means not to fix but to use our bloody raw pigments and sexual angst and suppressed novo-Cain rage, no longer for killing our brothers and sisters but for creating a novel work of art: like Van Gogh's *Sunflowers*, like Michelangelo's painting of the Sistine Chapel ceiling, like Victor Hugo's *Les Misérables*—to bless the cosmos for generations yet to come?

I extend an invitation now to allow the torn photographic scraps of your own Jacoblike dysfunctional family or church systems, present or past—your manipulation of others or allowing yourself to be manipulated; a wound created from an overly dominative or overly passive parent—to be integrated into a new collage of male soul power. Because if you surrender these torn negatives, bit by bit, to the Light in the photographic darkroom of prayer, the falling-rising Christ will become incarnate in your own life.

For this reconciliation of Esau and Jacob to occur within our own souls and in relation to others, we need courage to develop the skills and use the tools to reconcile *the feeling of power* with *the power of feeling.*

## PRAYER EXERCISE 14: Jacob Embraces Esau

Read and meditate on the text of Genesis 33:1-11, using Resource I, Praying with Scripture—personal *lectio*. If you are in a group, use Resource II, Scripture Sharing—group *lectio*, and be attentive to the third step, which calls you to some action that might embrace another person or group different from yourself. (Conclude by rereading "Warrior Lover Twins" on page 115–116.)

## PRAYER EXERCISE 15: Joseph Welcomes His Brothers

Read over the text of Genesis 45:1-5. Prayerfully allow a person from your own life to come to mind with whom you desire a healing of relationship. (It may be someone living, someone who has died, or someone with whom it is impossible to meet with physically.) (1) Close your eyes, and begin to picture the person. Begin to repeat the phrase, "Come closer to me" (45:4). Do not force anything; just allow yourself to hear the words. At first they may be your words to the other person; then they may become his or her words to you; and finally they seem to be God's words to you. (2) Notice if there are areas of that person's life that may be important for you to embrace—good qualities or gifts, even if the relationship has been strained. Use your journal to reflect or carry on an inner dialogue.

## For Personal Reflection or Group Conversation

1.  Reflect on the reconciling embraces between Jacob and Esau, Joseph and his brothers, and the Prodigal and his father. What are the obstacles to our expressing genuine affection?

2.  What are some areas that beckon you as most strongly in need of reconciliation within your own soul? between other individuals? among social groups?

## RESTSTOP 4:
## Grieving an Absent Father—Healing Holograms

Many young men are being reared by single mothers—the father literally being absent, or present infrequently at best. In a powerful story from Victor Hugo's novel, *Les Misérables*, a simple gesture of hospitality from one person in a church pew becomes the bearer of a life-altering experience.

Young Marius is grieving the death of the father he never knew. He has been separated from his father since childhood because of divided family politics regarding the French Revolution. In his grief, something draws him to return to Saint Sulpice Church in Paris, where his aunt had taken him as a child.

Being a bit more absentminded than usual, kneeling down, he takes his place behind a pillar, before he notices a velvet chair bearing the inscription: *Monsieur Mabeuf, Churchwarden*. No sooner had the mass begun than an old man interrupted Marius: "Monsieur, this is my place." Marius moved.

After mass, the old man spoke to Marius apologetically. He was sorry for having interrupted Marius, but it seemed to him the mass is better from that seat. Why? Because, for over a decade, he had watched "a poor brave father" who had sat in that very seat. It seemed the man could find no other way of seeing his child, being prevented through some family arrangements. The warden continued, describing the man:

> He came at the hour when he knew his son was brought to mass. He looked at his child, and wept. This poor man worshipped this little boy. I saw that. This place has become sanctified, as it were, for me, and I have acquired the habit of coming here to hear the mass. I was even acquainted slightly with this unfortunate gentleman. He had a father-in-law, a rich aunt, relatives, I do not remember exactly, who threatened to disinherit the child if he, the father, should see him. He had sacrificed himself that his son might some day be rich and happy. They were separated by political opinions. . . . Bless me! because a man was at Waterloo he is not a monster; a father is not separated from his child for that. He was one of Bonaparte's colonels. He is dead, I believe. He lived at

Vernon, where my brother is curé, and his name is something like Pontmarie, Montpercy. He had a handsome sabre cut.

"Pontmercy," said Marius, turning pale.

"Exactly; Pontmercy. Did you know him?"

"Monsieur," said Marius, "he was my father."

The old churchwarden clasped his hands, and exclaimed—"Ah! you are the child! Yes, that is it; he ought to be a man now. Well poor child, you can say that you had a father who loved you well."[2]

Here is a retroactive healing for the young Marius. A churchwarden's simple gesture of hospitality in speaking to Marius became a "service" of reconciliation for a man grieving a father he never knew. Such a healing hologram arrives unforced, serendipitous.

One night I dreamed of a man with whom I had a painful relationship in a church where I was pastor. By reflecting in my journal I came to see how he had been used for good in my life. Some years later, I met him at a summer concert and felt a deep love for him—and felt his response in kind. The next day we embraced with tears.

Like the experience of Marius, a single such reconciliation can represent a healing hologram for an entire web of conflicted relationships. We need to be attentive to these serendipitous openings for grace.

# Skills for Journeymen
## Qualities for Male Mentors

> There is a great difference between the skill and the grace of prayer. The skill consists chiefly in a readiness of thought consistent with various aspects of prayer. . . . The grace consists in the inward workings of the heart and conscience toward God and our life of faith.
>
> —Isaac Watts

There are five skills or "spiritual aptitudes" that journeymen need to cultivate so that our feeling of power can embrace the power of feeling: soul fitness; empowered listening; balancing sabbath and action; healthy intimacy with our brothers—and sisters; and creative use of "negative" emotions and experiences. After describing these five skills, in the two chapters that follow I will highlight tools for our vocation—ten specific practices to nurture these spiritual aptitudes.

### Five Journeymen Qualities

#### 1. Soul Fitness

Everyone understands physical fitness, but by soul fitness I refer to the Hebrew concept for soul or *nefesh*, which includes one's whole being—body, mind, and spirit. You could call it integrative spirituality. *Soul fitness means attending to the need for healthy self-nurturance in every sphere of one's life because there is no separation of sacred and secular.* Jesus exemplified this integration, and when asked which Commandment was the greatest, quoted the *Shema*, named for the first word of the verse in Hebrew, meaning "hear" or "listen." "The first is, 'Hear, O Israel: the Lord our God, the Lord is one; you shall love the Lord your God with all your heart, and with all your soul, and with all your mind, and with all your strength [with all your being].' The second is this, 'You shall love your neighbor as yourself'" (Mark 12:29-31; and see Deut. 6:4-5; Lev. 19:18).

## 2. Empowered Listening

To live out the command to love God, neighbor, and self is to begin with its first word, *Shema*: Listen to Love to love. It means listening beneath the surface of your life. Listen to how deeply God loves you in your woundedness and your giftedness, for only with a hearing heart can you really love another. (See Prayer Exercise 7, Option.) Empowered listening affirms self and others, freeing us to love rather control. It is both active and comtemplative. Active listening focuses on validating another's feelings before responding. *Contemplative listening adds the dimension of pausing to ask what God might be saying to you through a brother or sister.* Sometimes the best response may be no answer, but merely the gift of allowing another to be heard or receiving an insight yourself instead of giving one.

Such listening comes hard for us. A man told me of his father's advice as he grew up: "Don't come to me with a problem unless you already have a solution." This haunting inner voice wreaked havoc with his career and his relationships; he could not really listen to a problem without simultaneously solving it. It is a universal example of the male wound in one specific life. It is this mindset always to have answers that closes us to God and keeps us from being vulnerable enough to listen or ask questions—which might save us from our own wrong answers and build friendships at the same time. As Mark Twain reportedly said, "It's not what you don't know that gets you in trouble, but what you think you know that ain't true."

Males, who value the power of our own bodies, need to practice body awareness as we listen. A dismissive tilt of one's head, a thoughtless gesture can close another person down. An open posture and focused attentiveness empowers mutual listening. Practices of contemplative prayer promote this open spiritual posture—and can keep us from letting our own body abuse another. (See Tools in chapter 11.)

## 3. Balancing Sabbath and Action

The genuine male soul, one that is not captive to the false buzz of the world, is one that embraces a healthy passiveness and a healthy assertiveness. It is one that discerns the appropriate equilibrium of resting and risk taking, being held like a lamb (extradependence) going forth to lead the flock (intradependence). It is one that has learned the art of empowered listening, which can happen only in Sabbath, because Sabbath is all about being still.

Cultivating Sabbath spaces is the skill of pulling back from our tendency to control, at the same time unlocking the authentic power of impoverished feelings instead of walling them off in our noncommunicative caves. *It is the radical skill of recognizing creative gifts that come out of emptiness, wilderness, and bewilderment.* In the ancient wisdom of the rabbis, the purpose of Sabbath is to pray and to play.

Inventors and scientists have understood this truth and incorporated it into their lives. Friedrich August Kekulé von Stradonitz discovered the theory of "the benzene ring" not in the chemistry laboratory but while dozing in a state of semiconsciousness by his fireplace after dinner; Einstein said that imagination (which comes out of "wasted" daydreaming) is more important than knowledge.

The contrast of bright and dark pigments creates chiaroscuro, so essential in Rembrandt's paintings and Matthew B. Brady's Civil War photography. We need this essential skill of blending the gifts of silence and speech, solitude and community.

Musicians build this concept into the structure of a symphony. A theme is stated early on. Then comes a "something else"—a Sabbath, so to speak, a very different sort of sound, so that when the theme returns, the "something else" has allowed the original theme to be implanted in our memory. Likewise, Sabbath pauses for silence and retreat can return us to the original theme of our life's mission.

When I was in seminary, the week before the comprehensive exam in church history I designed and built a dry sink that still houses our stereo! Such simple projects can create practical healing for our everyday stresses. When I come upon a block in writing, I often think of the "something else" metaphor, then take some time to pray and play: woodworking, biking, playing the piano, cooking a meal, or reading. Then on returning to the task, new thoughts will bubble up.

This innate rhythm of involvement and withdrawal is built into our biological selves, but it is seriously threatened by our overdeveloped lifestyle.

## 4. Healthy Intimacy with Our Brothers—and Sisters

Cultivating healthy intimacy with God is the key to healthy intimacy with self and others. As Jesus illustrated by the summary of the Law, *when God's love permeates the whole of your life then your soul becomes more lovingly permeable to your brothers—and sisters.* I put the two in this sequence because I am convinced that working on our barriers as sons, brothers, and fathers is essential for creating healthy relationships with women.

For both men and women, Jesus models a radical new kind of family ("My mother and my brothers are those who hear the word of God and do it," Luke 8:21).

In relation to men, Jesus often confronts success ("Go, sell what you have, and give to the poor"), affirms male creativity ("The master commended the dishonest steward for his shrewdness"), and sides with the poor man over the rich, the tax collector over the Pharisee. (See Mark 10:21; Luke 16:8, 16:19-31, 18:9-14, RSV.)

In relation to women, Jesus exercises freedom from maternal ties ("Woman, what have you to do with me?"), defends the vulnerable ("Why do you trouble the woman?"), validates the intellectual rights of women ("Mary, who sat at the Lord's feet and listened to his teaching"), affirms women's authority ("Do not hold me, . . . but go to my brethren") and honors the feelings shared with him. (See John 2:4, Matt. 26:10, Luke 10:39, John 20:17, RSV.)

In each set of examples, Jesus is inviting us as men to open our vulnerable selves to God and each other, and to honor our own feminine or shadow side. We can trust this Messiah to defend and anoint us with spiritual authority far more authentic than macho domination. We are released from the burden of always being a *perfect* example to the freedom of being a *genuine* example.

What gets in the way of developing this mutual trust and vulnerability? In one word, grief. A friend of mine is working on a doctoral thesis asserting that most American literary heroes are either physical or spiritual orphans because we have all been cut off from our roots. We are exiled from our true selves, and our anger, angst, and addictions become the products we market to each other to cover up our deepest fears. (See Spiritual Friendship, chapter 12.) Like the primal creation in Genesis, without self-expression a person remains in deep chaos: "Give sorrow words. The grief that does not speak / Whispers the o'er-fraught heart and bids it break" (Shakespeare, *Macbeth*,

IV.iii). Without the language of love, we regress into spiritual chaos, because violence is the language of the inarticulate.[1]

The unique connection with male spirituality is that we are culturally trained to deny our grief, to mask our pain and pretend it is not there. But only if we become aware of our pain can we really embrace it and offer it to God. And only if we offer it to God can it be transformed—the ultimate spiritual aptitude.

> A leaf that has served its purpose
> as a thing of beauty
> can only become
> nurturing
> humus
> when it
> leaves:
> detaching
> as it grieves,
> it fails and falls
> to the Ground of its being
> to nurture another thing of beauty.[2]

## 5. Creative Use of "Negative" Experiences

*The deep mystery of God's underground grace can take even raw shame and abuse and transform it into life-giving resiliency.* Frederick Douglass, a child slave who would become a brilliant educator, had overheard his master forbidding that Douglass learn to read or write. This made Douglass so determined to master the alphabet that he chose to subject himself to being shamed. Through keen observation he had learned four letters, and he boasted that he could draw them better than white boys. They taunted him, "Betcha you don't know the next letter!" He would endure their shaming until he had tricked yet another letter out of his youthful oppressors, finally winning the treasure that would be his doorway to new life.

It is this mindset that Paul describes in an early Christian hymn about Christ's self-emptying (Greek *kenōsis*) as the paradoxical prelude to resurrection and new life (Phil. 2:1-11). This *kenōsis* mindset is the upside-down message of Jesus: "Blessed are the poor in spirit." "The last will be first."

Humor is born out of the lowest places in life and is related to human, humility, and humus. Many comedians developed humor as their ally because as kids they were lonely or physically weak. People laugh and cry when reading about the Irish misery in Frank McCourt's bestseller *Angela's Ashes*. Genuine male humor is deeper than imported jokes. A teacher who formerly redesigned the F-117 stealth fighter used to order people to almost certain death. Now in the classroom, nothing is obeyed blindly. His only choice is to use humor instead of pulling rank. Humor can create "power from below," far more effective than fear-based commands.

And when this happens it is truly *sublime*, and sublimation is not suppression. This is a radical internal skill where even irreversible shame can become a gift if we embrace it and offer it, just as Jesus surrendered at the cross: "Abba, into your hands I commend my spirit" (Luke 23:46, AT). (See chapter 5 on transforming anger.) The "mystery of Christ" transforms brokenness into blessing (Eph. 3:9-10). We can never grow beyond the paschal mystery, only deepen it.

## Masculine Stumbling Blocks: Channels for Underground Grace

I have presented numerous stories illustrating the truth that our wounds can be metamorphosed into a gift for the community. Now I propose that even our masculine stumbling blocks to prayer can be disguised invitations to a deeper life with God, channels for underground grace.

### What If . . .

Our pre-occupations stuff an empty hunger
  for the only One who can occupy our distorted longings?
Our withholding camouflages our yearning
  for the hidden God?
Our controlling masks our desperate longing
  for a sovereign God?
Our overanalyzing is a human plea for God
  to make sense out of the daily blitz of suffering?
Our impatience with trivial routines reflects a yearning
  for meaning beyond the trivial?
Our addictions to work, sex, and chemicals are lures
  toward the Treasure beyond our pleasures?
Our misplaced anger and violence are our primal scream
  to penetrate the silence of One whose address we have lost?

"Our heart is restless till it finds its rest in you," we pray with Augustine of Hippo.

There are two contrasting ways of viewing these so-called "negative" and "masculine" qualities. A male-bashing approach views these male obstacles to the Divine as demons to be exorcised, "when really they might be angels of annunciation," as Anne Morrow Lindbergh wrote in *Gift from the Sea*. So I am proposing a gospel-like alternative: that these same "negative" characteristics can be disguised pointers to God.[3] What if we can find ways to meet God through the mundane and even the profane?

Clearly I am not approving of traits like male domination and violence. What I am saying is that, as in the story of *Beauty and the Beast*, our brute behaviors are only outward symptoms of a deeper gnawing fear. What would it mean to befriend the beast? to befriend the anger? to befriend the fear beneath the anger? "There is no fear in love, but perfect love casts out fear" (1 John 4:18). If, Jacoblike and Esaulike, we could find ways to turn around and embrace the enemy parts of our soul—that would be a profound kind of repentance.

Tools for Journeymen, the subjects of the next two chapters, are methods to help us listen beneath the surface of our control, our anger, our analysis, and our addictions as channels for underground grace.

## PRAYER EXERCISE 16: Assessing Your Spiritual Skills

Using your journal, list and assess the five qualities journeymen need to cultivate as they relate to your own personality and experiences. What aspects are you feeling called to deepen? Which of the five do others affirm in you? Converse with yourself and God about gifts and needs in each area. Then find someone or a group with whom you can reflect on your insights.

## For Personal Reflection or Group Conversation

1. Reflect on qualities for mentors, which you listed at the end of chapter 7. How do these compare with the five skills (qualities) the author develops in this chapter?

2. If the ultimate spiritual skill is to develop the art of using negative experiences for positive purpose, what would that look like in your life? Conclude by composing a brief written prayer.

# EXCURSION 6:
# FYI: Analyzing Data, Synthesizing Life

## FYI

For Your Information:
analyze the data
but more important
synthesize life.

Both Goethe and Kierkegaard remind us that synthesis and analysis must alternate as naturally as breathing in and breathing out. We guys tend to be good at analyzing stuff, finding out why, figuring things out. And "out" is our male anatomical bent, a tendency given in nature and a habit reinforced from nurture.

In a society of shallow breathers addicted to "output," no wonder one of the original Hebrew meanings of the word *shâbat* is "to catch one's breath"! Sabbath is all about allowing time to synthesize, to make life-giving connections. In an age of overinformation and overspecialization, who will synthesize the arts and sciences, poetry and prose, psychology and economics? Who will make prophetic connections between the sexual spirituality of mystical poets like John Donne with the sex industry of Hollywood and Madison Avenue? Donne was right too: "No man is an island." If we fail to make such connections, we die isolated on a trillion islands.

Silence and spiritual retreat are essential if journeymen are to be genuine mentors for the next supersaturated generation. (See Silence and Retreat, chapter 11.) Synthesis functions like the sinews and connective tissues of the human body—and when they break down life cannot endure. It is not coincidental that the words *ligament* and *religion* come from the same Latin word *ligare*, meaning "to bind, to tie," and that is what the ministry of reconciliation is all about (2 Cor. 5:14-21). It is a call to join in Abigail's powerful prayer for King David, that "the life [of our world] may be bound in the bundle of the living under the care of the LORD your God" (1 Sam. 25:29).

My prayer is that men, who in this century have been the primary builders of incredible weapons of human and environmental destruction, will in the next century be the pioneers in binding our fractured world together.

Of course, just as surely as we bind up the wounded, there comes a time when the bandages for one generation constrict the next, when tired religious rituals need new wineskins. Then, like Jesus' calling Lazarus forth from the tomb—feet bound and face wrapped, the word of the Lord is: "Unbind him, and let him go" (John 11:44).

The skilled journeyman is called to the prophetic rhythm of binding up and unbinding, discerning when to analyze and when to synthesize—"to pluck up and pull down, . . . to build and to plant" (Jer. 1:10).

But this is not just abstract or "churchy" stuff. In a society heavy on analysis, synthesis can save lives in our compartmentalized educational, industrial, economic, and medical institutions. I just returned from a Gershwin concert by pianist Richard Glazier. He told of George Gershwin's fatal brain tumor at age thirty-eight in 1937. Everyone, including his brother Ira, thought George's symptoms were due to "nerves"—symptoms like smelling burning rubber, later recognized as a sign of the tumor. Months went by, but surgery came too late. Yet Gershwin's fatal brain tumor resulted in a medical benchmark. Now a consultation is required between psychological and neurological assessments in such cases—a triumph of synthesis redemptively using analysis.

A primary purpose of worship in our time is to synthesize life— to help folks who work all week long in highly specialized areas to discover healthy connections with each other and God.

# Tools of the Trade

## Five Essentials for
## Healthy Male Solitude

> Only in the fellowship do we learn to be rightly alone and
> only in the aloneness do we learn to live rightly in the fellow-
> ship. It is not as though one preceded the other; both begin at
> the same time, namely, with the call of Jesus Christ.
>
> —Dietrich Bonhoeffer, *Life Together*

Clicking on my computer "Tools," I find spiritual parallels: "Language" (the community of faith is where you learn the language
of love); "Auto Summarize" and "Track Changes" (a journal tracks
themes and changes in your spiritual journey); "Auto Correct" (con-
fession assists frequent midcourse corrections); "Customize" and
"Options" (find the best spiritual tools for your unique personality);
"Menu" and "Table" (you are invited to a soul feast); "Internet"
(prayer connects you with a global spiritual network). The tools often
seem complicated but are designed as simple ways to access the incredible hidden potential of this nine-by-twelve-inch plastic box (prayer
practices are nothing in themselves but they access our incredible
God-potential).

The term *tools of the trade* is also meant to convey a mutual
exchange—personal renewal, service in the world. This abbreviated
list of spiritual disciplines is compact enough to take with you on your
day journeys, like the portable tool chest I take when I work with

Habitat for Humanity. These ten tools put flesh on the five skills to nurture an integrated male soul. I recommend deeper reading for each area where you find yourself drawn. (See also chapter 5.)

I have classified them in two broad categories: five disciplines of solitude (chapter 11), and five disciplines of community (chapter 12). Although I view community as foundational, in this case I start with solitude since men often find it a likelier place to begin, or begin again. As tools of the trade, each needs the exchange with the other five.

Here are five practical ways to quiet the overactive male soul so that, cocoonlike, transformation can take place all the time: (1) an honest personal prayer life—including physical exercises, scriptures, journaling, centering prayer, and prayers and music of others; (2) spiritual readings; (3) nature and silence; (4) a life mission statement; and (5) discernment. They are practices to promote *kenōsis*, the habit of self-emptying—to create Sabbath space "to listen to Love to love." They are bridges to lure us to the Holy through the profane and the mundane. But they are merely the conduits to tap the flow of underground grace.

## Disciplines of Solitude

### 1. An Honest Personal Prayer Life

The model for "honest to God praying" is the Book of Psalms, the prayerbook of the Bible. The Psalms reflect all the moods of the soul from anger to despair to joy and include the use of physical movement and breathing—poetry, music, silence, dance, nature. "Pray always, pray all ways"; the goal of disciplined times for daily prayer (Hebrew *keva*) is to develop an attitude of prayerful involvement throughout the day (*kavanah*). Two other minimal disciplines:

- Aim for prayer on a daily basis, but keep the actual ratio to at least four days out of seven, for a period of half an hour to an hour.

- Promise at least two minutes of silence each morning to center yourself, no matter how late you get up or how busy you are— even if you cannot keep your set-aside period of prayer, or will keep it later. In a dark period of my life, this habit sustained me for months as I sat, head drooped, after putting my shoes on.

Each of the following methods can be adapted to a ratio of prayer in relation to oneself and others.

a) *Physical and spiritual exercises.* Though you may vary your sequence, for males there's some logic in beginning with physical praying. As one young man said to me, "I need to honor my reptilian self." Newsmagazines proclaim that "men worship their bodies," so it feels good to begin by worshiping God with my body! (Rom. 12:1-3). Walking or jogging while listening to music or meditating on a scripture, doing some routine of tai chi or yoga, or your own blend of "body prayer" movements—all while being attentive to your breathing—are good ways to open the soul to God. Two decades ago I began to combine physical and spiritual exercises while doing prescribed exercises for my back. I found I could incorporate repeated scriptures and intercessions—praying the Lord's Prayer to sit-ups, inwardly singing lines of hymns to body stretches, and so on. It is incarnational spirituality. Even for not-so-athletic guys like myself, gentle forms of movement have been powerful forms for me to yoke the spiritual and physical—the meaning of "yoga." (When I climbed Mount Kenya recently, my guide said it had paid off!) Praying with the body makes me attentive if I am drowsy, or it relaxes my over-energetic self, readying me for silence.

b) *Praying with scripture.* Start with silence to open the heart and mind. The ancient Benedictine practice of *lectio divina* or prayerful reading (as outlined by Guigo II in the twelfth century) is a good way to allow the Word to become flesh in the particular stuff of your own life. This one tool is recommended and can be adapted for all sixteen Myers-Briggs Personality Types (See 5. on page 139): (1) Reading, like a cow grazing; (2) Meditating, like a cow chewing; (3)Praying, like a cow ruminating; (4) Contemplating, like a cow resting, digesting.

Three options for praying with scriptures assist our apprenticing: (1) Visualize the scene in a narrative text; (2) converse with the various characters—like the wounded man, the robbers, the priest, the Levite, the Good Samaritan, then with Jesus or God (inwardly, or using a journal); (3) repeat a short phrase that lures you, like a centering prayer. Keep your journal and Bible with you during personal prayer times since the two will feed each other. (See Resource I, Praying with Scripture—Personal *Lectio*; also Resource II, Scripture Sharing—Group *Lectio*.)

c) *Keeping a journal.* Writing reflections on experiences in a journal will integrate each isolated *jour* (day) with your lifelong *journey.* Dag Hammarskjöld's *Markings,* Henri J. M. Nouwen's *The Genesee Diary,* and Reinhold Niebuhr's *Leaves from the Notebook of a Tamed Cynic* are classic examples.

Many men have kept a diary to record mere data: "Went to the Farmers Market at 4 PM Saw Todd." As a skilled journeyman you keep a journal to record your spiritual response to the data: "Went to the Farmers Market at 4 PM Saw Todd, who just lost his job. I reflected on my own career changes. . . . It drew me to pray for him. . . ." Try journaling in response to scripture; conversations with others; life experiences; quotations; readings, lectures or sermons; dreams; poetry, art, or music (your own, or others'); meditations or prayer exercises, such as some in this book or in my book *Active Spirituality,* or in Anthony de Mello's *Sadhana: A Way to God: Christian Exercises in Eastern Form.* Be creative and practical. "Art" your dream symbols or scripture images; write a thought during the day on a Post-It note and stick it in your journal at night.

d) *Centering prayer and silent contemplation.* The use of a repeated word or phrase in rhythm to one's breathing has a long tradition for centering the soul on the active journey. Normally a simple word is best, such as "Abba," or "Manna," or "Shalom," or the longer Prayer of the Heart or Jesus Prayer: "Lord Jesus Christ, Son of God [inhaling], have mercy on me, a sinner [exhaling]." You can pray a short scripture text as a centering prayer: "Let there be light," which can also used a repeated prayer for intercessions as they come to mind. (See Gen. 1:2.) Or pray with Psalm 46:10: "Be still [breathing in], and know that I am God! [breathing out]." And that is the purpose of centering prayer—to still the soul. It is the first rung on the ladder of contemplative prayer. After a few minutes, let go of the phrase, and stay in a posture of loving and being loved, as the hymn says, "lost in wonder, love and praise."

e) *The prayers and music of others.* A Lutheran pastor once told me, "When I can't pray, the church helps me." Hymns and prayers of others can be channels for underground grace. Your boss does not have to know you are praying or singing inside your head—as Benjamin Weir and Terry Waite did when held hostage in Lebanon.

As I do body stretches, inwardly I sing a thirteenth-century prayer of Richard of Chichester to a tune from the musical *Godspell:*

"Day by day, O dear Lord, three things I pray, to see thee more clearly, love thee more dearly, follow thee more nearly, day by day." I pray the Serenity Prayer (made popular by the Twelve-Step groups) with exercises for my back: "God, grant me the serenity to accept the things I cannot change, the courage to change the things I can, and the wisdom to know the difference." *A Guide to Prayer for All God's People*, edited by Rueben P. Job and Norman Shawchuck, contains a treasury of prayers, hymns—and spiritual readings, our next topic.

## 2. Spiritual Readings

More men than women score high on "thinking"—compared to "feeling" on the MBTI (Myers Briggs Type Indicator). So like C. S. Lewis, nurturing the mind is one of our primary spiritual paths. Yet I choose not to include much spiritual reading in my personal prayer time, because it often means shortchanging the silence and contemplation that are so crucial and undervalued. Rather I suggest choosing other times during the week to nurture the soul with words and ideas. Of course prayer exercises or brief quotations often do become grist of personal prayer, and books are grist for communal study groups or longer-term training programs. Apprenticing surely means knowing the principles and practices of past and present mentors if we are not to slip and slide on the path.

## 3. Nature, Silence, and Retreat

Once in a workshop I invited people to just five minutes of silence. An accountant reported that he had gone in his mind to Villa d'Este in Italy—the silence had brought back a visual experience and sounds of waterfalls in the beautiful palaces. It shows that by emptying external stimulation we can tap rich internal resources. It also illustrates two classic ways of experiencing God. The kataphatic path or via positiva moves *toward* the world—through sound, words, art, music, ideas, action. The apophatic path or via negativa moves *away* from the world—through silence, night, retreat, wordless contemplation. So often nature is a bridge between these two. We see this double pattern as Jesus ministers in crowded cities and celebrations, then retreats into mountains or wilderness in silence.

I am issuing a clarion call for active men, young and old, to take time apart for an overnight and day retreat at least twice a year. Ask a Catholic friend where there is a monastery or retreat center close to nature. Or trek into real wilderness. Do not take a stack of books, only your Bible and a journal. Go alone or with a friend, but be attentive to nature and keep silence till returning home. Work with your church to set up a quiet day a few times a year, possibly right in the church building. Work to build in a ratio of silence into the next youth retreat, men's retreat, Sunday school class, church council, or small-group meeting. Action needs silence. Incredibly, the two can become one, as when Jesus' silence before Pilate became a political act.

In *The Violence of Love*, Oscar Romero, the martyred archbishop of San Salvador, tells of being asked by a journalist what kept him going despite so many threats on his life. Answering that he was just back from another spiritual retreat, he added: "If it were not for this prayer and reflection, I would not be more than what Saint Paul says, 'clanging metal.'"

### 4. A Life Mission Statement

Jesus said, "If your eye is single, your whole body will be full of light" (Matt. 6:22, AP). This single focus for your life creates the healing of purpose as I wrote about in chapter 6. Your mission statement is your "why" for living—the only reason for engaging in healthy habits of the heart. It is your unique expression of what it means for you to listen to Love to love. From Stephen R. Covey in *The Seven Habits of Highly Effective People* to Richard N. Bolles in *What Color Is Your Parachute?* a lot has been written on the value of this tool. But the point is not to write a lot, but rather a few words to complete the sentence: "I am here on this earth to . . ."

Let your mission statement reflect a twofold focus: your own gifts (what puts a sparkle in your eyes?) and some concern of the world (what pulls at your heartstrings?). Seneca said, "Without knowing which port one is sailing toward, there is no such thing as a favorable wind" (AT). Your mission statement is a way to practice discernment—to see the connections between your destinations and God's destiny.

> Guide us all on this day journey,
> Poor yet privileged by your grace,
> To experience life incredible, fragile,
> While on earth this little space.
> —*Guide Us All on This Day Journey*

## 5. Practicing Discernment

There are four tools for discerning how to respond to God in the world: (a) Excellent practical tools for discernment of one's unique gifts and skills are contemporary personality-type instruments such as the Myers-Briggs Type Indicator (MBTI) based on Jungian archetypes, and (b) the Enneagram, an ancient tool recently made popular and "Christianized," especially by persons like Richard Rohr, a Franciscan. (c) The process for discernment developed by Ignatius of Loyola in *The Spiritual Exercises* is an invaluable tool for listening simultaneously to the world and to God.[1] (d) The Clearness Committee of the Quaker tradition is a practical method for a small group of men (or a mixed group) to focus on another journeyman's sense of call and response. Though it draws on community, the Clearness Committee is a tool for personal discernment and is initiated by an individual "focus person" seeking clearness. (See Prayer Exercise 18.)

Of course, discernment is also a corporate discipline, as when a large body of people try to discern the Spirit's leading on issues of faith and life. Acts 15 provides a biblical example: "The whole assembly kept silence," and "It has seemed good to the Holy Spirit and to us to impose on you no further burden than these essentials" (Acts 15:12, 28). This is what the Quakers call "the sense of the meeting," and silence is its key ingredient. We will explore these corporate disciplines in chapter 12.

## PRAYER EXERCISE 17: Redesigning Your Prayer Time

I invite you to take three pages in a journal, and at the top of each list the following: *barriers* that get in the way of your creating an intentional time for personal prayer; *benefits* you know to be of value for yourself from this practice; and *bridges* to solitude—methods of prayer to assist your soul in coming home to your true self and God.

After prayerfully assessing these three areas, you will get the most value from this exercise by sharing your responses one-on-one with another person.

NOTE: Some would urge you to try methods that seem to fit your own personality type: "Pray as you can, and not as you can't." I attach the addendum, "Yes, but until you try some ways you think you can't pray, you don't know quite so well how you can!"

FOR GROUP USE: After sharing in pairs, the leader may gather and record responses from the group, enriching each other's appreciation for various needs and practices.

## PRAYER EXERCISE 18: The Clearness Committee

Originally developed by the Friends for discernment when two persons want to be married, the Clearness Committee is adapted now for individuals facing a variety of vocational struggles. A support group of likeminded people might offer to be available for each other—though the person seeking clearness may also choose participants from other contexts of life.

The person seeking clearness writes up his or her situation in advance and circulates it to five or six trusted persons whom he or she invites, asking one to serve as convener, another as notetaker. The meeting begins with centering prayer and silence, then a fresh statement of the concern by the focus person. This is followed by silence, then by discerning questions: "Have you considered . . . ?"—but not "fix-it" advice, "Why don't you . . . ?"—and observations: "I'm hearing four possible careers. . . ." All is in a prayerful atmosphere, and may end with "the laying on of hands" in prayer. The group may be reconvened.[2]

OPTION: The mission statement would make an excellent ingredient for reflection with a Clearness Committee.

## For Personal Reflection or Group Conversation

1.  "The goal of disciplined times for daily prayer (Hebrew *keva*) is to develop an attitude of prayerful involvement throughout the day (*kavanah*)." What does this ratio look like in your life?

2.  What are some of the forms of practicing your prayerfulness throughout the day?

3.  Using Prayer Exercise 17, reflect with another person or a group: What are the obstacles and growth edges of prayer in your life?

## RESTSTOP 5:
## Blacksmith Road—The Journey to Being Soulsmiths

I live on Blacksmith Road, but who even knows a smith of any kind—blacksmith, tinsmith, silversmith, locksmith? A smith is one who skillfully "smites" raw hot metal, using a forge, anvil, and hammer, and shapes it to fit an intended need, creating a utensil that is both beautiful and practical.

A real smith is rare today, though the name is still widespread. *Journeymen* is a plea to people the world with smiths again: word*smiths*, communication*smiths*, sound*smiths*, relation*smiths*, law*smiths*, economic-*smiths*, environment*smiths*, peace*smiths*—soul*smiths*.

Soulsmiths are apprenticed to use the tools of the Spirit to craft the raw materials of life to fit the needs of our time. When someone is "smitten" with fear or grief or love, we who are soulsmiths have learned the art of taking the blows and using our skill and strength to help our sisters and brothers shape it for a practical and beautiful use in the world. It is an arty and gritty business.

Dietrich Bonhoeffer practiced his trade while imprisoned by the Nazis for protesting the Holocaust, writing reflections in his *Letters and Papers from Prison*. Attached to one of Bonhoeffer's prison prayers are these words from a mentor pastor and mystic, Gerhard Tersteegen: "Each day tells the other / My life is but a journey / to a great and endless life."[3] The art of previous apprentices sustained him in times of doubt.

For journeymen, our faith is hammered on the anvil of doubt. The trade has entered our body, blow by blow. We are now apprenticed to trade our gifts with everyone—men, women, and youth. Our vocation is to call all people to practice the art of being soulsmiths: to use the tools of the Spirit to craft the raw materials of life to fit the needs of our time. This book is a call to people the world with soulsmiths.

# 12

# Tools of the Trade
## Five Essentials for
## Healthy Male Community

But we enjoyed playing games and were punished for them by men who played games themselves. However, grown-up games are known as "business," and even though boys' games are much the same, they are punished for them by their elders. No one pities either the boys or the men, though surely we deserved pity.

—Saint Augustine, *Confessions*

I, miserable painter that I am, have painted a portrait of an ideal man; and here I have been directing others to the shore of perfection, I, who am still tossed about on the waves of sin. But in the shipwreck of this life, sustain me, I beseech you, with the plank of your prayers, so that, as my weight is sinking down, you may uplift me with your meritorious hand.

—Saint Gregory the Great, *Pastoral Care*

Without the discipline of community, solitude degenerates into self-absorption and isolation; without the discipline of solitude, community degenerates into codependency and enmeshment. In chapter 11 we discovered five tools or disciplines of solitude. Here are five more tools to help us discern, to rid us of the clutter we use to stuff our longings: (1) a life-giving faith community; (2) family relationships—tools for singles, couples, and parents; (3) spiritual friends and mentors; (4) a support group; and (5) life-giving stories.

We need the community for a creative exchange of these "tools of the trade." Some of these may seem like "old saws," but if we sharpen them and use them wisely they can cut right through the distractions that keep us from seeing God in ordinary people and circumstances:

> We're companions on a perilous journey
> Finding Love while being found.

But to be found by this incredible Love we need companions.

## Disciplines for Life with Others

### 1. A Life-giving Faith Community

Guys can be rugged individualists, so we need to listen to John Wesley: "There is no such thing as a solitary Christian." The community of faith is where we learn the language of love. And the church uses two kinds of language—the verbal language of liturgy, scripture, and sermon, and the body language of sacraments, gestures, and social outreach. The ultimate form of body prayer is to immerse oneself in "the body of Christ" where one's own gifts can be multiplied incredibly (Rom. 12; 1 Cor. 12). An electrician who had given me rich insights into the meaning of *journeymen* exhibited an inner longing for his life to make a difference beyond day-to-day work. I told him the story of a builder who taught a Sunday school class; of a tree surgeon who served as a Big Brother for city kids; of a self-educated airline mechanic who played the guitar and was a trusted church youth advisor; of former United States President Jimmy Carter volunteering with Habitat for Humanity.

Being part of a life-giving faith community is like a healthy foot getting directional signals from the rest of the body. A life-giving church is one where human brokenness is lifted up like bread and wine to be held, and touched, and blessed—to heal the world. A life-giving church fosters small groups—microchurches within the macrochurch to nurture family relationships, spiritual friendship, support groups—all bound together by life-giving stories.

If you are not part of such a transforming, life-giving organism—pray to discover one, or pray and work to change the one you are in, with love.

## 2. Family Relationships

The journeymen's goal is empowering love, and a man's role in a family is to encourage the spiritual leadership of each member. With phone and e-mail it is possible to promote networking with family members at a distance to offset the dilemma of families that are sadly cut off from older generations. Jesus blesses a new kind of family: "My mother and my brothers are those who hear the word of God and do it" (Luke 8:21). It is a message of freedom and invitation to single-parent and blended families in our time to "adopt" grandparents and aunts and uncles—and the church is a ready-made family formation center.

Rituals and stories create the essential glue for a collage of family spirituality, a renewed family system where we are free to become the unique selves we are meant to be. (See Resource III, Faith Finding, Faith-Sharing.) We need a positive word for men (and women) who are singles, couples, and for any who dare to take on the role of parents. All three types need to interact with each other because all of us need time alone and time with others.

a) *Singling.* This word is meant to convey the necessity for each of us to become an independent self somewhere along the way, so that we do not get ourselves enmeshed in unhealthy coupling and parenting. Jesus was referring to this need for spiritual individuality when he made the strange statement that unless you "hate" your father and mother you cannot be a disciple (Luke 14:26). No one dare write about men and family without underscoring that persons who are single or single again are a part of the new kind of family as Jesus defines it.

My wife is an only child and my only sibling died young, and we were both born of older parents. So while our children were still young, their grandparents died and they had no aunts and uncles. The celebrations of our little nuclear family have regularly included an older single cousin, a couple with no children who are "aunt and uncle," and countless singles, old and young. Our churches need to set the example for an inclusive attitude in the macrocosm of corporate worship and in the microcosm of classes and committees, small groups, and family activities.

Disciplines of solitude (chapter 11) are a key to healthy spiritual individuation, developing positive regard for being single, and positive love relationships.

b) *Coupling.* I have advocated shared household tasks to engender sexual intimacy because outward behaviors and contemplative listening are two sides of the coin of healthy feelings between lovers. (See Reststop 3.) But when separated from each other by circumstances, divorce, or death, each of us needs to have cultivated a healthy, intact soul. The journeyman practices his trade by using the art of creative trade-offs in any healthy marriage or relationship.

When I am out of town, my wife has created significant friendships by inviting other women to concerts and plays; I have done the same by inviting guys to movies she has seen already or does not want to see. Each of us follows a unique spiritual path while sharing mutual gifts—all with enough trust to leave a lot of things unresolved. Here is a call for couples to encourage each other to cultivate unique gifts and friendships apart from each other.

Instead of a verbal grace or prayers, the frequent Quakerlike ritual of allowing several minutes of silence (sharing afterward what each of us was pondering) allows space for uniqueness, and creates intimacy during the silence and the sharing. (See Prayer Exercise 19.)

c) *Parenting.* I often quip that when I was in seminary, I had three theories of child rearing, but now that I have three children, I have no theories left! I used to bug our older daughter to practice her cello. Then, I vividly recall, one day she turned to me and said, "All right, Dad, if you keep saying that, I'll quit. But if you let me alone, maybe I'll practice, maybe not as much as you want." Parenting is a matter of discerning the time for urging on and the time for pulling back (Eccl. 3:1-11). As I ponder that fragile moment of *kenōsis*, of pulling back, today it is sheer joy! As I write this, she has just moved from the University of Pennsylvania in Philadelphia to Asheville, North Carolina, to begin her three-year medical residency. She has taken her cello with her.

These are mentoring moments for the mentor, if one allows them to be, slow, upside-down epiphanies. And there are on-the-spot epiphanies, too. Our son, at age four from Korea and in the United States only a few months, was asked by an agnostic relative, "Was anyone with you on the airplane?" The answer was instant, "Yes, Jesus." Where had that come from? In a holy moment of *kenōsis* everyone fell silent.

But poet Wendell Berry is right:

> For parents, the only way
> is hard. We who give life
> give pain. And there is no help.
> Yet we who give pain
> give love; by pain we learn
> the extremity of love.[1]

Late-night phone calls, listening to one's anorectic pain, to another from the streets of San Francisco, I have learned to embrace the sleeplessness as a kind of prayer without words, praying in my gut, yearning with "bowels and mercies" (Phil. 2:1, KJV).

And what of the pain of my friend whose wife died of leukemia in her thirties? As a single male parent he tells me of bonding with his young son but of struggling to relate to his daughter as she begins to face the new and scary experiences of young womanhood. Yet he also tells me of his supportive office community—other staff picking his kids up from school, women reaching out to his daughter. "By pain we learn / the extremity of love."

In my young fathering I was helped by Charlie Shedd's books on sex education and his cassette series Fun Family Forum. Around the family table, we would each share "the most interesting thing" that had happened in the past twenty-four hours.

I began a ritual of taking each child out alone to eat—which settled into report-card time, or now whenever one of them comes home. Those conversations reflect a thousand variations on two simple questions in Prayer Exercise 19, Share and Prayer with a Child—What's something that's going well for you? What's something that has you a bit concerned? I had to share, too, from the perspective of what was going on in my life. Taking my turn at putting the kids to bed, I would subtly vary the same exercise.

But now with the three in their twenties, the only theology that helps is that of providence: "Honor your father and your mother" becomes a command for me to honor God as the only reliable Parent—who will fight for our kids and who will hold them in the arms of love (Exod. 20:12; Deut. 1:30-31). And this is the same God who redeems my distorted parenting and that of my own parents— who also fights for me and holds me.

3. Spiritual Friendship—spiritual mentoring

On retiring, a man told how his work buddies had requested, "Keep in touch now." He waited a few months, and one morning he phoned one, then another. Each greeted him eagerly, "Great to hear from you, Joe!" But when he would suggest lunch or golf, the conversations abruptly ended—they had pressing obligations with present colleagues and clients.

This pathetic story is repeated daily. Saint Augustine was right: "Grown-up games are known as 'business' . . . No one pities either the boys or the men, though surely we deserved pity." No wonder my nephew, who as a teen spent his summers with us after my brother died, would turn up the radio to Elton John's "Sad Songs." A thousand country singers croon away about a woman who betrayed, or a guy down on his luck, but not about our grief for failing to be our brother's brothers. Like Cain, we kill our Abel brothers, only more subtly.

Of course women have more long-term friends than men. But what does that fact mean? What is the invitation for us? Sometimes it means going back and rekindling an adolescent friendship, or reconciling with a midlife "enemy." It seems like a divine joke that men, traditionally not letter writers, are primary users of e-mail! Granted, in e-mail you cannot read the feelings between the lines, but I have used e-mail to initiate both rekindlings and reconcilings.

Other times it means *carpe diem*—to "seize the day" and deepen the friendships at your fingertips now. But always it means having the courage to be vulnerable: "I have called you friends, because I have made known to you everything" (John 15:15). Christ meets you on the road where you are now. Cultivating friendship with God (chapter 11) will surely open up friendships with some stranger on the same road—who may be the Messiah in disguise (Luke 24:13-35). "Always moving in upon [one's] life is the friend whose existence [one] did not know, whose coming and going is not [one's] to determine," wrote Howard Thurman in *The Inward Journey*.

There are two specific invitations here. One is to look for spiritual friendships at your fingertips, within your own faith circle, where you intentionally seek God with another soul. The other is to prayerfully seek out cross-cultural human friendships beyond the circle of your own experience.

a) Spiritual friendship is what the Irish call *anamchara*, soul friends. This kind of one-on-one friendship is not task-related. Aelred of Rievaulx in twelfth-century England literally wrote the book on it, *Spiritual Friendship*.

> What joy to have someone to whom you dare to speak on terms of equality as to another self; one to whom you need have no fear to confess your failings; one to whom you can unblushingly make known what progress you have made in the spiritual life; one to whom you can entrust all the secrets of your heart and before whom you can place all your plans!

Such a friend, Aelred continues, "is the medicine of life." Spiritual companionship is a gentle process of faith finding and faith sharing. Anyone can meet with another Christian friend and share stories of doubt and faith and struggles and blessings—and sit in silence and pray together. Ideally, you find a person who can be your spiritual mentor, primarily a listener and responder, and then you also serve as a spiritual mentor for another one or more persons, formally or informally. Usually you would meet monthly. You could use a book like this one as a source for spiritual conversation and prayer exercises. In the more formal sense it is called *spiritual direction*, and there are training programs and literature for it.

b) For Esau to embrace Jacob means you reach out to someone outside your familiar circle, who is really a brother (or sister). Contact your local church or any denominational headquarters to get information about a cross-cultural mission trip; encourage others to engage in such contemporary mission pilgrimages as an alternative to cruises and tours. Locally, pray to seek out friends from other ethnic traditions— go to their center of worship; invite someone to speak at your church, to set up a dialogue series for Lent, to go out for lunch, to break bread in your home. Share your faith stories, and listen to those of others. Begin a dialogue on e-mail with someone you met at a conference. If we are to love our neighbor, we will first need to listen to our neighbor.

Christ calls us from being strangers to ourselves and others to becoming friends embraced in the arc of divine Friendship. I am blessed when I look at my "personal board of directors" and at their variety since I have begun to pray and think this way. (See Prayer Exercise 12.)

## 4. A Spiritual Support Group

*Either find or found a support group*—people with similar vocational, personal, or family struggles. To such groups I owe my survival, growth, and many friendships during twenty years in parishes and ten years of a specialized ministry. "It is not good that the man should be alone" is not just God's counsel that primitive Adam needed a spouse. *It means it is not healthy for any man to bear his problems alone.* And any loved one who bears all of one man's problems alone will burn out, or else both will clam up and bury their hurts. Every man needs a safe space that is life giving, health producing, and spiritually nurturing. (See Resource IV, A Model for a Men's Group.)

To find or found a group may mean starting with just one other person. The form can vary, but it is essential to keep three rules: confidentiality, honesty, and commitment—to be present, to be culturally inclusive, and to keep each other in prayer. If the group expands beyond six, then build in at least ten minutes for spiritual friendship in pairs or groups of four. This serves many purposes. It is safer for the introvert to share with one other person—guys are not likely to share depth of feeling with a large group—and timewise, you give each person more "air time" this way.

Typically local church men's groups fall into four categories: breakfast eaters, fund raisers, Promise Keepers, or "drum beaters"—groups using the mythic-poetic approach like Robert Bly's *Iron John*. Sometimes these groups also function as the kind of spiritual support group I am speaking about; other times it is best to begin with a small group with its own clear agenda.

Here is an invitation for churches to form men's spiritual support groups—call them "Journeymen"—with an eye to creating friendships that bridge cultural, geographical, and economic barriers. Here is a plea for us to enter into spiritual support groups that move beyond a Lone Ranger way of life and adopt the standards of journeymen: *radical honesty, spiritual vulnerability, and cultural inclusiveness.* No more powerful example exists than the Twelve-Step groups like Alcoholics Anonymous. And the key to these groups, like Aelred's description of spiritual friendship, will be listening to each other's experiences or doubt and faith, the ancient art of storytelling.

## 5. Life-giving Stories

I have been advocating that we find ways for men to connect their feeling of power with the power of feeling, ways to move from a dominative stance that makes others feel impoverished to a creative stance of empowering love. But it is intimidating for men to be asked directly to tell "how you feel" to a group.

This is what I have found to be the key: *If a man can feel supported and safe enough to revisit an experience of life and put it into a story, he will drop beneath his jokes to express feelings of joy, pride, and gratitude. He will drop beneath his anger to express feelings of grief, regret, or shame.* The story's the means by which we discover the man's countenance.

But how do you encourage men to get in touch with their own stories? Newscaster Edward R. Murrow used to take his listening audience to the immediacy of an event by using his favorite line: "And you are there." Telling a "you are there" experience drops us down beneath our generic head statements ("Just gotta grin and bear it; stuff happens; everybody's got their cross to bear; life just isn't fair"). When a guy makes such statements, ask him: "Can you take me to some moment in your life where you experienced [whatever it is he's just said]?" Then get the courage to use the G word: "What do you think God might be trying to say to you through that experience [of pain or joy]?" You may be amazed at the response.

"By pain we learn / the extremity of love," and if we can encourage each other to feel safe enough to go to the extremes of our lives—deep pain or deep joy—then by reliving such experiences, we can see God become palpably present in our church basements, locker rooms, board rooms, and family rooms. Stories that come from the raw places of life and are lifted up, like the serpent on the pole, become life-giving.

Scientific studies have shown that stories simultaneously stimulate activity in both the right brain—creating images, feelings, senses, *and* the left brain—using linear, sequential data, developing a "story line." So they are good bridge skills for thinking and feeling types, women, men, and children.

Stories can check our tendency to give advice. As poet Mary Oliver has written in *House of Light*, "There are so many stories / more beautiful than answers." Jesus understood this; Lincoln understood this. It is what Emily Dickinson meant when she said, "Tell all the truth but tell it slant." If you believe even our profane or mundane experiences can be the conduit for underground grace, then you will never dismiss anyone's story as trivial. (See Resource III, "Faith Finding, Faith Sharing.")

## PRAYER EXERCISE 19: Prayers for Singles, Couples, and Parents

### Open-Eyed Grace

This grace can be used at home (alone or with others) or church gatherings, before or during a meal. Leader: "Become aware of our unity with all others and creation, breathing in the same air that rich and poor breathe around the globe. Smell the smells, notice the colors, contemplate the food in front of you. . . . Visualize the dark soil, the bright sun . . . the farmers who planted it . . . the migrant farm laborers who picked it with their hands. Now gently lift *your* hands as intercession on their behalf, with thanks. Conclude by saying the word *Gracias!* three times in unison—a Spanish word that conveys both grace for those in need and thanks!"

### Share and Prayer with a Child

This exercise uses two basic questions: What is something good happening in your life now? (or, in our relationship?) Then—What is something that has you a little bit anxious or concerned? (or, something you would like to see changed?) The adult has to take a turn, too; then both pray together, silently or aloud, saying to God what each just said to the other. The exercise can be used as bedtime prayers, or adapted when out to eat, one-on-one.

OPTION: This can be an enriching ritual for couples, or for singles with another friend.

### Silent Couple Prayer

Instead of a verbal grace or prayers, try the Quakerlike ritual of allowing several minutes of silence. Then share afterward what each partner was pondering and praying. This allows space for uniqueness, yet creates intimacy during the silence, and in the sharing.

OPTION: While (or after) discussing a difficult issue, pause for this kind of silence. The sharing that follows changes the tone, and often brings clarity to the issue.

## PRAYER EXERCISE 20: Cross-cultural Friendship (Personal or Group Use)

Read the text of John 15:12-15, about servants and friends. As you use the personal or group *lectio* (Resource I or II) to pray with this text, be particularly attentive to a person or group of persons different from yourself with whom you would like to become friends. Spend some time meditating and praying for yourself and the other(s). If ideas come to you during the praying, jot them down in your journal. Then put everything aside. Spend some time in silent contemplation, knowing that you and the other(s) are known and loved by God.

IDEA: Put a Post-It note a few pages ahead in your journal with a written reminder to ask yourself: How am I praying about [name of desire]?

## For Personal Reflection or Group Conversation

1.  Reflect on Prayer Exercise 20 with another person or with a group. What are the barriers to cross-cultural friendships for you?

2.  What are the barriers to genuine self-disclosure in cross-cultural relationships? between men and other men?

3.  If you are single, what are some of the issues that make it difficult to be open with others who are not single? If you are married, what are some of the barriers to your including single people in your context of family and church? (Make sure to invite a single person as part of this discussion, one-on-one, or in a group.)

4.  There are times as mentors or parents you must pull back from your most treasured values to allow space for those same values to arise in the ones you love. (See chapter 7.) In your relationships, what helps you to discern the time for urging on and the time for pulling back?

# EXCURSION 7:
## Global Journeymen—A Day at a Time

Webster's unabridged dictionary of the English Language defines a journeyman as (1) "a person who has served an apprenticeship at a trade or handicraft and is certified to work at it. . . ." (2) "any experienced, competent but routine worker or performer." (3) "a person [who works] for another usually for a day at a time." From this we can harvest more insights.

Be global journeymen.

Ancient journeymen contracted for jobs within a day's travel from their own village. You can see the word "day" in "*journey*" (*jour*, in French, is "day"). *Journey* is derived from the Old French *journée* and the Latin *diurnus* ("daily"), and "journey" originally referred to the distance one could travel in a day's time. Amazingly, today with electronic communication and methods of monetary exchange you can literally practice your trade around the whole world and come back in one day without even leaving your own home!

Here is a plea to use our technology as tools for the Spirit to be global journeymen. I have a friend, who when the institution he worked for downsized, was not fazed at all. He went to India on a subsistence income where he teaches computer science in a Christian school. But you do not need to go to India—although you may.

Through intercessory prayer any of us can travel around the world and connect on a spiritual Internet, all from home. And intercessory prayer can take many alternative forms: faxing, e-mailing, writing your congresspersons—or a friend in Kenya or England; writing a check to the Sierra Club, the Cousteau Society, your local church's food pantry, or a homeless project.

A journeyman practices the art of being present by proxy on the streets of the global village. A journeyman practices the art of trading his gifts to bridge the frightening gap between those who are materially poor but spiritually rich—and most of us who are materially rich but spiritually poor. We can use the tools of technology as tools of the Spirit and to practice the craft of global trading.

Live one day at a time.

*Day* can also refer to one's whole life: morning (youth); noon (midlife); afternoon (elder years); and night (death). So the craft of a skilled journeyperson is to live one's whole life one day at a time. It is the motto of the Twelve-Step groups. It is central to the life and message of Jesus: "Do not be anxious about tomorrow. . . . Let the day's own trouble be sufficient for the day" (Matt. 6:34, RSV).

Practice your routine work as a holy vocation.

It is the classic wisdom of Brother Lawrence in *Practicing the Presence of God* that the simplest task is a holy vocation. In the words of the fifties singer Charlie King, "Our life is more than our work and our work is more than our job." Journeypersons have been apprenticed to live by the wisdom attributed to Mother Ann Lee of the Shakers: "Do your work as if you had a thousand years to live; do your work as if you were to die tomorrow."

And as Webster's puts it, our trade is always "for Another": "Take my yoke upon you, and learn from me." And it is being there for others. Journeymen are soulsmiths mentoring other soulsmiths—women, men, and youth.

> Guide us all on this day journey,
> Poor yet privileged by your grace,
> To experience life incredible, fragile,
> While on earth this little space.
>
> We're companions on a perilous journey
> Finding Love while being found.
>
> —*Guide Us All on This Day Journey*

# Praying with Scripture
## Personal *Lectio Divina* Process

Many people think of their personal devotional life consisting of reading the Bible, then saying their prayers. This is an exercise where the two come together: *praying the scriptures*. In the fifth century, Benedict of Nursia gave us a simple method: the *lectio divina*—the "divine" or "prayerful" reading of scriptures. Read a short text prayerfully—over and over, like a cow chewing her cud—until you are led to "delight in God." In the twelfth century, Guigo II divided Benedict's *Lectio* into a fourfold experience, beginning with silence:

1. Reading: like a cow grazing, use a lectionary or other method to select and read a brief portion of scripture silently, aloud—or both ways;

2. Meditating: like a cow chewing, reread it, ponder the context—allow meanings and associations to come to mind;

3. Praying: like a cow regurgitating its sour cud, ruminate on the text, let it get down in your gut and connect with your raw feelings;

4. Contemplating: like the cow resting, digesting—allow the Word you need to get into your bloodstream.

Contemplation is what the psalmist means by "Delight yourself in the LORD, and [God] will give you the desires of your heart" (Ps. 37:4, NIV). It is Luke's image of Mary sitting at the feet of Jesus, listening. Jesus "taught us to seek a retreat that would help us to descend into our heart. . . . That God . . . will be near to us in the affections of our hearts" (from John Calvin's *Institutes of the Christian Religion*, III, 20, 29). The Word becomes flesh in us embodied in service.

Three options for praying with scripture have been passed down through the centuries:

(a) Use the imagination to visualize a scene in a narrative text.

(b) Converse with the various characters. (Reflect inwardly, or using a journal).

(c) Repeat a short phrase that lures you, like a centering prayer. Keep a journal and Bible with you during personal prayer times.

# Scripture Sharing
## Group *Lectio Divina* Process

This method in monastic practice was called *collatio*, originally "bringing together" of a shared supper. It is a bringing together of friends and stories related to a scripture text. It is used in retreats, during lunchbreaks, and in "base communities" of developing countries where Bible study, prayer, singing, and personal and social change often merge. It is a unique way to create small group *koinōnia* even in a large gathering or space. (Allow at least a half hour.) Each person needs a Bible or printed text (ten verses maximum).

- LEADER OF LARGE GROUP: Briefly summarize the purpose and process; announce the text. Have participants form groups of four to seven, optimum (may be in same room); form a circle and sit close. Have each group designate a convener.

STEP 1. *"Listen for God's word as it touches your life—notice a word, phrase, or metaphor that 'shimmers'—lures you or unnerves you."*

- CONVENER IN EACH SMALL GROUP: Celebrate the presence of Christ—use a brief spoken prayer, a song or chant—focus on breathing, followed by silence.
- Repeat 1 above. Allow silence. Each may read silently first.
- Read the text aloud; may read again slowly. (*lectio*)
- Invite each person: "Begin to repeat a word or phrase silently, or if it is a metaphor or an image, visualize it." Allow a few minutes of quiet. (*meditatio*)
- Invite persons to "share a word, phrase, or metaphor that touches your life" without commenting on it.

STEP 2. *"Notice some feeling or experience in relation to the word, phrase, or metaphor."* (*oratio*—prayer)

- SECOND READING: Convener (or another person) reads the text aloud again, slowly.
- Invite each person to share a second time, reflecting on some feeling or experience.

(Accept sharing, usually without discussion; use *I, me*—avoid *we, us, you*; keep confidentiality; be comfortable with silence; listen, receiving another's story as a gift.)

STEP 3. *Ask: "What is God inviting me to do or be this week? Am I being called to some action—now in this setting, in my relationships with family, work, leisure?"*

(Before the third reading, announce if the group has an extended time, Option A or B, below.)

- THIRD READING: Convener (or another person) reads text aloud a third time.

A: Take an extended time for reflection, journaling, art, movement, or other ways of praying. Announce time to return. Persons may stay or leave as they are ready, keeping silence.

B: Move directly from the third reading (after a brief silence) to sharing discoveries.

- Return to group(s). Invite persons to share any beckonings to action or decision.

STEP 4. End with unison prayer and/or song (may return to large group if several small groups), and a period of silence, loving God and being loved. (*contemplatio*)

OTHER OPTIONS:

(a) Invite each to offer a free prayer for the person on your right, in light of what the person shared (or to offer a prayer silently, then say an "amen" as cue for the next person); continue around the group. Thank persons on right and left for their prayers!

(b) Sing a prayer: *Kum Ba Yah . . . Someone's praying*—invite thanksgivings in a word or phrase . . .; *Someone's crying*—invite intercessions . . .; *Someone's singing*—stand, raise arms in joy!

# Faith Finding, Faith Sharing
## For Use in Church, over Lunch, in Homes, at Work

LEADER: Briefly summarize this exercise and explain its purpose: to connect faith with daily life. It is faith sharing "from below," so each person stands on an equal footing.

"Choose someone with whom you will share in a few minutes—turn to the person next to you, or all get up and mix around until everyone is linked with someone." (Invite everyone to be seated; create a quite atmosphere. Then announce:)

STEP 1. "Think over the past week (or period of time), and notice a problem you've had to confront." (Allow a few minutes of silence.)

STEP 2. "Contemplate: How has God—or Christ, or prayer, or your faith, or your community of faith—made a difference in how you responded to that problem?" (Allow a few minutes of silence. Then find a simple way to break the silence: a spoken "amen," ringing a soft bell, or a sentence prayer such as, "O God, be with us now as we share.")

STEP 3. "Meet with one other person and share the issue or concern. Reflect with your neighbor on how your faith made a difference." (Announce length of time for sharing—six to ten minutes total; three to five minutes per person. After sharing, invite each pair now to spend one minute in silent prayer.)

STEP 4. "Closing your eyes, picture the face of your partner, lifting up that person's needs and gifts." (Option: "Offer a sentence prayer for each other.") "When you are ready, give your friend some sign of Christ's peace." (Then end with some large-group discussion, asking:) "What did we learn about faith sharing?" (Conclude with a hymn or a spiritual—such as "Guide My Feet," "Amazing Grace," or "Day By Day.")

See Resource IV, A Model for a Men's Group.

# A Model for a Men's Group
## Journeymen: Guidelines for Spiritual Apprentices and Mentors

PURPOSE: Either find or found a men's spiritual support group made up of members with similar vocational, personal, or family struggles. A major focus is discernment: to support each other in making choices that best express love.

RATIONALE: Every man needs a safe space that is life giving, health producing, and spiritually nurturing. Without it we bury our feelings or overburden those closest to us.

GROUND RULES: To find or found a group may mean starting with just one other person. Whatever the format, it is essential to keep these ground rules:
   1. Confidentiality—what is shared stays with the group;
   2. Honesty—"speak the truth in love," be real with each other;
   3. Commitment—be present or accounted for, be culturally inclusive, and keep each other in prayer.
   4. Agree to a specific starting and ending time.
   If the group expands beyond six, then build in at least ten minutes for spiritual friendship one-on-one (or in groups of four to six). This serves many purposes. It is a safer way for the introvert to share; even extroverted men are not likely to share in depth with a larger group, and each person has more "air time" this way. Disadvantage: Not all get to hear every man's issues, but this can be offset. (See number 3 on page 161.)

PROCEDURES:
   1. Rotate the convener role.
   2. The convener is the timekeeper. (This is crucial; individuals may come early or stay after.)

FORMAT: The sequence and length for each item below may vary. The convener is responsible to lead or direct each of the following:

1. Five minutes of silence, preferably at the beginning, or later if you start with a group exercise (the convener may use a meditation or prayer exercise to lead into silence);

2. Ten to thirty minutes for mutual support using Faith Finding, Faith Sharing (Resource III, or an adaptation), Scripture Sharing (Resource II, group *lectio*), or any similar relational prayer exercise (in groups of two to six persons);

3. Ten minutes for intercessory prayer (for the entire group to hear brief concerns), for example, "For Craig, whose mother has cancer. . . ." "For the unrest in [name of a country] . . ." "For [oneself] for guidance at work . . ." etc. A very meaningful method is to sing a verse of a spiritual song (hymn or chant), then offer the concerns, and sing the song again; or use a scripture litany such as "Let there be light" after each one's concern. NOTE: This is the way to offset the problem of a large group. Having small groups earlier allows for each person to have shared in more depth, but this method allows the entire group to hear something of everyone's concerns.

4. Ten to thirty minutes for any individuals who are in need of specific guidance, healing, or support to make it known. For example, someone in need of discernment for work or family issues might ask for prayers to convene a Clearness Committee, asking a few in the group to participate. (See Prayer Exercise 18.) Or someone recently diagnosed with cancer might ask for prayer and the laying on of hands.

5. Choose the convener for next time.

LENGTH OF MEETINGS: The above components comfortably fit in an hour and a half (or two hours if including a book discussion).

FREQUENCY OF MEETINGS: Weekly, semimonthly, or monthly (minimum).

OPTIONAL BOOK STUDY (ten to twenty minutes): Since the purpose of these meetings is relational, it may be best for those who want a book study to offer it at a separate time, or less frequently, alternate weeks, etc.

OPTION: Everyone can be reading a book in common as background reading without formal discussion time.

# A Litany for Men
## With Prayers by and for All

LEADER (MALE): Peace be with you, brothers! (and sisters!—if joint gathering)

ALL: *And also with you.*

LEADER: We are men and we are many; we are apprentices and mentors.

MEN: God of all times and places, we see you more fully through our varied skin complexions, geographical locations, and vocations.

ALL: *Help us not to pin you down in one place, one race, or one way of life or work.* (Silence)

L: We are farmers and agriculturists, explorers and geologists.

M: We see you in newborn calves and dark soil, open skies and rock outcroppings.

A: *Help us cultivate your presence in all of life and blaze new trails.* (Silence)

L: We are builders and carpenters, architects and engineers.

M: We know you in the cedars and pines, the smell of sawdust, the fine lines on a drafting board.

A: *Help us to follow the design of the carpenter and builder of Nazareth.* (Silence)

L: We are teachers and musicians, coaches and athletes.

M: We see you in the best of team spirit, the insights of students, the harmony produced through discords of life.

A: *Help us to discipline ourselves, to do the hard work of practice that allows your gift within us to come forth.* (Silence)

L: We are physicians and healers, therapists and social workers.

M: We know you through the healing of the body.

A: *Help us join you in the process of becoming strong at the broken places.*
(Silence)

L: We are mechanics and plumbers, truckers and pilots, chefs and tailors.

M: We see you in the weld that's stronger than either side of the broken joint; we see you in the hospitality on the way, and that's as important as arriving at the destination.

A: *Help us to learn from the obstacles on the journey— to mend the torn fabric of the universe, to repair the broken transmission of the universe.* (Silence)

L: We are fathers and we are sons, we are boys and we are men.

M: We see you in the wrinkled memory of age and the prankish energy of a toddler, the forgetful repetition of old stories and the curious questions of Why this, Why that?

A: *Help us to keep turning to the Christ who said that we cannot see the commonwealth of heaven unless we come as a child, so to nurture the child within each of us and among all of us.* (Silence)

L: And now we turn to you, O God, like a mother eagle bearing her young upon her wings, you bear us and bring us to yourself; and we pray the family prayer:

A: *Our Father . . .* (using "sins")

# RESOURCE VI

# Guide Us All On This Day Journey

Words: Kent Ira Groff 1998

Music: Kent Ira Groff 1998

Words and Music Copyright 1998 by Kent Ira Groff

NOTE: To duplicate this song, contact Upper Room Books™ for permission.

# ENDNOTES

INTRODUCTION

1. This poem and all other poems, unless otherwise noted, are written by Kent Groff.

CHAPTER 1

1. Christiane Northrup, M.D., "Celebrating Feminine Energy in Healing: Embracing Gender Difference," lecture at Chautauqua Institution, July 12, 1996, highlights the relationship of heart attacks and hostility, career, and lifestyle. (New York: Chautauqua Institution, Cassette 96-55). See also Christiane Northrup, M.D., *Women's Bodies, Women's Wisdom: Creating Physical and Emotional Health and Healing* (New York: Bantam Books, 1998); and Mehmet Oz, M.D., Ron Arias, Lisa Oz, Dean Ornish, *Healing from the Heart: A Leading Heart Surgeon Explores the Cutting Edge of Alternative Medicine* (New York: E. P. Dutton, 1998).

2. Myriam Miedzian, *Boys Will Be Boys: Breaking the Link Between Masculinity and Violence* (New York: Anchor Books, 1991), 7.

3. There are some exceptions, where writers attempt to integrate the dimensions of Christian faith and men's literature: Patrick M. Arnold, *Wildmen, Warriors, and Kings: Masculine Spirituality and the Bible* (New York: Crossroad, 1995); Stephen B. Boyd, *The Men We Long To Be: Beyond Domination to New Christian Understanding of Manhood* (San Francisco: HarperSanFrancisco, 1995); Philip Culbertson, *New Adam: The Future of Male Spirituality* (Minneapolis, Minn.: Augsburg Fortress, 1992); and James E. Dittes, *Driven By Hope: Men and Meaning* (Louisville, Ky.: Westminster John Knox, 1996).

4. Roberta C. Bondi, *Memories of God: Theological Reflections on a Life* (Nashville, Tenn.: Abingdon, 1995); Diane Tennis, *Is God The Only Reliable Father?* (Philadelphia, Pa.: Westminster, 1985).

EXCURSION 1

5. Milan Kundera, *Immortality*, trans. Peter Kuss (New York: HarperPerennial, 1991), 223.

6. Admiral David Glasgow Farragut stated this at the Battle of Mobile Bay (August 5, 1864).

CHAPTER 2

1. Raymond Carver, "A Small Good Thing," from *Where I'm Coming From* in Paula J. Carlson & Peter S. Hawkins, eds., *Listening for God: Contemporary Literature and the Life of Faith*, Vol. 1 (Minneapolis, Minn.: Augsburg Fortress, 1994), 75–76.

CHAPTER 3

1. Evelyn Underhill, *The Spiritual Life* (Harrisburg, Pa.: Morehouse, 1997), 20.

2. Blaise Pascal, *Pensées*, in *Mind on Fire*, ed. James M. Houston (Minneapolis, Minn.: Bethany House, 1997), 109.

3. Alice Miller, *For Your Own Good: Hidden Cruelty in Child-Rearing and the Roots of Violence* (New York: Farrar, Straus & Giroux, 1983), 142–197.

CHAPTER 4

1. See Gordon Dalbey, *Sons of the Father: Healing the Father Wound in Men Today* (Wheaton, Ill.: Tyndale House, 1996), 17–19. On male withdrawal, also see Earl R. Henslin, *Man to Man* (Nashville, Tenn.: Thomas Nelson, 1993), 154–55.

2. See Tillie Olson, *Silences* (New York: Dell, 1978), 137–38.

EXCURSION 3

3. Kundera, *Immortality*, 194–95.

4. Flannery O'Connor, *Mystery and Manners: Occasional Prose* (New York: Farrar, Straus & Giroux, 1969), 132.

CHAPTER 6

1. Northrup, M.D., *Women's Bodies, Women's Wisdom: Creating Physical and Emotional Health and Healing* speaks of the need for balancing these emphases. See also Mehmet Oz, M.D., et al., *Healing from the Heart*. (See chapter 1, note 1).

2. Christiane Northrup, M.D., 601–04: "Respect and Release Your Emotions."

CHAPTER 7

1. J. D. Salinger, *The Catcher in the Rye* (Boston, Mass.: Little, Brown and Co., 1951), 246.

2. Thomas J. Watson Jr. and Peter Petre, *Father, Son & Co.* (New York: Bantam, 1990), 315.

3. *Ibid.*

4. Samuel Osherson, *Finding Our Fathers: How A Man's Life Is Shaped by His Relationship with His Father* (New York: Fawcett Columbine, 1986), 54.

5. *Ibid.*, 57.

6. Rainer Maria Rilke, *Letters to a Young Poet*, rev. ed.; trans. M. D. Herter Norton (New York: W. W. Norton, 1954) 35.

CHAPTER 8

1. *John of the Cross: Selected Writings*, ed. K. Kavanaugh, O.C.D. (New York: Paulist, 1987), 55–57.

2. *Ibid.*

3. *Ibid.*

4. See Mary Field Belenky, Blythe McVicker Clinchy, Nancy Rule Goldberger, and Jill Mattuck Tarule, *Women's Ways of Knowing: The Development of Self, Voice, and Mind* (San Francisco: BasicBooks, 1986).

5. *The Essential Gandhi: An Anthology of His Life, Work and Ideas*, ed. Louis Fischer (New York: Random House, 1983), 35–37.

CHAPTER 9

1. Arthur Conan Doyle, "The Adventure of the Three Garridebs" in *The Case Book of Sherlock Holmes* (New York: Book-of-the-Month Club, 1994), 167.

RESTSTOP 4

2. Victor Hugo, *Les Misérables*, trans. Charles E. Wilbour, abr. James K. Robinson (New York: Ballantine, 1961), 144–145.

CHAPTER 10

1. "Violence is the language of the inarticulate": Quotation from Bernard Lafayette Jr., Director of the Martin Luther King Jr. Center for Nonviolence, speaking at Chautauqua Institution, New York, July 1991.

2. This poem is reprinted from Kent Ira Groff, *Active Spirituality: A Guide for Seekers and Ministers* (Bethesda, Md.: The Alban Institute, 1993), 14.

3. I am indebted to James E. Dittes for this basic idea in *Driven By Hope: Men and Meaning*, viii.

CHAPTER 11

1. For a summary of the Ignatian discernment process, see Kent Ira Groff, *Active Spirituality*, chapter 20.

2. See Parker J. Palmer, "The Clearness Committee," *Weavings*, no. 4 (1988): 37–40.

RESTSTOP 5

3. Dietrich Bonhoeffer, *Letters and Papers from Prison*, ed. Eberhard Bethge (New York: Macmillan, 1971), 142.

CHAPTER 12

1. Wendell Berry, *Collected Poems: 1957–1982* (New York: North Point, 1995), 210.

# About the Author

Kent Ira Groff, an ordained Presbyterian minister, is founder and director of Oasis Ministries for Spiritual Development. Oasis Ministries is an interdenominational, nonprofit corporation that exists to renew the spiritual life of individuals, congregations, and institutions through retreats, spiritual direction, and training programs. He is also adjunct professor at Lancaster Theological Seminary in Pennsylvania.

The author has served as a parish pastor, chaplain, and in leadership positions in churches and organizations. Dr. Groff holds degrees from Pennsylvania State University (Bachelor of Arts), Princeton Theological Seminary (Master of Divinity), and Chicago Theological Seminary (Doctor of Religion). He is also a graduate of Shalem Institute for Spiritual Formation in Washington, D.C., and he completed his chaplain residency at University Hospital, Hershey Medical Center of Pennsylvania State University.

Dr. Groff is the author of *Active Spirituality: A Guide for Seekers and Ministers* and other books, and has published numerous articles in religious periodicals. He also writes poetry and composes music. He is married to Fredrika Simpson Groff and they have three adult children: James, Kendra, and Elizabeth.

You may schedule retreats or contact the author at Oasis Ministries, 419 Deerfield Road, Camp Hill, Pennsylvania 17011.